7 Steps to Develop
HEALTHY RELATIONSHIPS
With Anyone

James Justin

Dedication

This book is dedicated to my wife, Dr. Lauretta Justin. You are the love of my life! You are my best friend, my inspiration and my sexy butterfly. Without you I would not be who I am, and this book would not be a reality. Thank you for challenging me to think bigger and pursue my goals. I love you always!

To my three sons: Nathan, Sean and Joshua Justin. Thank you for teaching me the true meaning of patience. Remember, together we will make a difference in the world! I love you!

Acknowledgement

I want to thank my parents for their guidance, love and support. I am eternally grateful to you, Mom and Dad! Thank you for your sacrifices and moving from Haiti to the United States of America to give me better opportunities to succeed and strive!

A special thank you to my editor and friend, Mark Wahlton! This book is a reality because of your brilliance. Thank you for being a valuable partner!

Products by James Justin

- Positive Parenting: 12 Practical Tips to Prepare your Kids for Success

- 7 Steps to Develop Healthy Relationships with Anyone

- 12 Tips to Achieve Financial Freedom: The Simple Guide to Successfully Manage your Personal Finance

- Mindset: How to Transform your Life from Ordinary to Extraordinary

- The Power of Prayer

Visit CoachJamesJustin.com to get all the products by the author!

Contents

Introduction

According to the American Psychologist Abraham Maslow, humans have a deep-seated need for belonging and acceptance within their social groups. These groups may be large or small. Large social groups can include co-workers, religious groups and professional organizations. Some examples of small social groups can include significant others, families and friends.

> **In order to learn how to build a healthy relationship, it is important to understand what a healthy relationship is.**

We have a very strong need to be loved by each other both sexually and non-sexually. If this significant need is not met, the results can be catastrophic. Medical conditions such as depression, anxiety and even suicide have all been linked to loneliness, hopelessness and a lack of acceptance by others.

In this day and age, we do not lack social groups. As a matter of fact, we have access to a plethora of social groups available to us 24/7 through social media. There are more clubs, organizations and social media groups now than ever before in history. Humans have more opportunities than ever to connect with each other through advanced technology. Yet, even with all these opportunities for connection, it seems people are feeling lonelier.

In a recent article from Forbes Magazine, I read the following: "Recent studies have found that despite being more connected than ever, more people feel more alone than ever." We do not have a lack of relationship opportunities. What we have is a lack of healthy relationships. This book is designed to equip you with the foundation for building healthy relationships with the people in your lives. As you build healthy relationships, you will fulfill your need for love and connection. Ultimately, building healthy relationships will result in a happier you.

A healthy relationship is characterized as a relationship that is of personal significance and mutual benefit, trust and respect.

There are many kinds of relationships, and each one has its own purpose. For example, my relationship with my wife serves a different purpose than my relationships with my business partners, friends and colleagues. My wife and I are in a lifelong committed partnership; whereas the commitment to relationships with my business partners, team members and clients is temporary. Regardless of the type of relationship, all relationships are important. Furthermore, all relationships must be founded on certain basic principles in order to succeed. This book is designed to teach you how to develop healthy relationships by following the seven steps outlined in these pages. These steps will give you the foundation to build a healthy relationship with anyone in your life.

A healthy relationship is characterized as a relationship that is of personal significance and mutual benefit, trust and respect. It is not one that is free from challenges, but one where the involved parties know how to *manage* the challenges. They understand how to use life's challenges as opportunities to improve and strengthen the relationship.

There are many benefits to healthy relationships. When two people are involved in a healthy relationship, each member is a winner. Healthy relationships add value to all involved parties. Healthy relationship is loving, caring and trusting. In a healthy relationship, each member is *celebrated* rather than *tolerated*.

> **In a healthy relationship, each member is *celebrated* rather than *tolerated*.**

The benefits of being in healthy relationships are numerous, and I have peppered them throughout this book. I can assure you that the benefits of being in healthy relationships are far greater than that of unhealthy relationships.

The primary reason for writing this book is to empower you to develop healthy relationships. As a minister, life coach and psychotherapist, I am aware of the major challenges people face in their dogged pursuit of what they perceive as healthy relationships. I know that the divorce rate in our country is higher now than decades ago.

About one generation ago, there were nine divorces out of every 1,000 marriages in the United States. According to *divorcepad.com*, the current divorce rate in the United States is now 50 percent. This alarming statistic, coupled with my observations of people suffering from unhealthy relationships compelled me to write this book. I want to inspire, empower and help people to take actions toward building better relationships. I want to promote a positive change in the world.

I believe that the steps outlined in this book will equip you with the tools required to build healthy relationships. These steps have changed my relationships and my life. I have been studying and researching the subject of relationships for more than 20 years. The lessons I have learned are presented in this book. If you study and practice the seven steps, your life will be changed as well.

> **People generally develop healthy relationships with those who are compatible, available, reliable and dependable.**

My journey to obtain and maintain healthy relationships began at the age of 14. I observed and asked people about their relationship experiences. I pondered on what they said to me and meditated on them as often as possible. My passion to understand people—how they think and how they interact with others in relationships—led me to pursue two college degrees in the field of counseling.

In my quest to learn more about relationships, I learned several lessons. One of these lessons is that people generally develop healthy relationships with those who are Compatible, Available, Reliable and Dependable (CARD). Most people feel they can trust those who possess these qualities. Do you possess the CARD qualities? If not, you may want to get a head start if you are serious about building healthy relationships, by developing those qualities. You can choose to develop these qualities in your efforts to pursue healthy relationships with anyone you want.

> **The health of your relationships will determine your level of success in life.**

If you are ready to pursue healthy relationships, you can start today by practicing the seven steps to healthy relationships as you encounter them throughout the book. When you engage in healthy relationships, it is a matter of personal choice. Nobody can force you to develop and maintain a relationship against your will. You have the power to develop and maintain the relationships your heart desires. The success of your relationships is founded on your willingness to work for what you want. However, I advise you to choose wisely, because your relationships will determine your level of success in life.

I invite you to embark on the journey to pursue healthy relationships. The benefits are worthwhile. Life is already so complicated; simplify it by developing healthy relationships. I have enjoyed the benefits of being in healthy relationships for years, and I hope for nothing less than the same for you!

Are you ready to develop healthy relationships? Let's get started with the Justin's 7 Steps to Healthy Relationships:

Step 1. Become Self-Aware

Step 2. Become Selective

Step 3. Become the Friend You Want to Attract

Step 4. Become an Effective Communicator

Step 5. Become Loving

Step 6. Become Trustworthy

Step 7. Become Committed

Step 1

Become Self-Aware

Self-awareness is about knowing who you are. It's the foundation of personal growth and development. When you know yourself, you are better prepared to understand people. The more you understand yourself, the more you can develop healthier relationships with anyone you desire.

> *"Getting to know yourself is a journey down the Yellow Brick Road to success and happiness."*
> Unknown

Daniel Goleman, the American Psychologist and author of "Emotional Intelligence," calls self-awareness the "keystone" of emotional intelligence. Emotional intelligence is your ability to identify and manage your own emotions and the emotions of others. As you discover how to understand and manage your emotions, you'll have greater understanding of yourself and others. When you are self-aware, you'll have the power to develop yourself and to develop healthier relationships.

No one can truly know another without first knowing themselves. In any relationship, you can only offer who you are and what you have. That is why we need to become self-aware to develop healthy relationships with anyone we want. Self-awareness is important in building healthy relationships because when you know yourself, you'll be in a better position to know and accept others as they truly are. Self-awareness is vital in all relationships because without such understanding it is nearly impossible to develop *healthy* relationships with the people in your life.

> **In any relationship, you can only offer who you are and what you have.**

The goal of this step is to help you get better acquainted with yourself in order to build healthier relationships. *If you do not know who you are, it will be difficult to know another.* In this step, you will be presented with a general overview of self-awareness, with the following concepts:

- The meaning of self-awareness
- 3 benefits of self-awareness
- 3 tips to improve your self-awareness

What is self-awareness?

Self-awareness is the process of understanding one's thoughts, feelings, actions and interpersonal connections with oneself and others. It is an honest assessment of who you believe you are. It is *"An awareness of one's own personality or individuality"*

(Merriam-Webster Dictionary). Self-awareness, as described by the American Psychological Association is *"The top level of consciousness; cognizance of the autobiographical character of personally experienced events."* In other words, it's your understanding and control of how your thoughts and feelings lead to your actions.

Self-awareness is important in building healthy relationships because of the control it gives us over our lives. When we know and understand how and why we react to certain events, we can manage ourselves better. I cannot improve what you don't know or understand.

For example, one of my sons used to carry his favorite trains with him everywhere he went. Sometimes, he'd carry five trains in his hands. They were always falling on the floor and we'd have to stop to pick them up. This irritated me every time. Sometimes I'd get so mad that I'd take them away. He would cry whenever I'd tell him he could not have his trains, or could only bring one train to our trips together.

> **Self-awareness is important because it gives us control over our lives.**

Then one day he cried so hard that it touched my heart. I thought about why it bothered me so much. Is there anything wrong with him carrying his favorite trains? He wasn't hurting anyone, so why was I so upset? After thinking and processing this with my wife, I realized that my anger was not toward the behavior or my son. It was toward what the behavior represented. You see, my son is diagnosed with autism, and every time he carried those trains, I was reminded that he was different, and that made me angry. It turned out that my frustration had nothing to do with the trains; I was angry about the fact of my son's situation.

Once I understood my son's condition and how its reality affected me, it helped me deal with my emotions. More importantly, our relationship improved tremendously. I allowed him to bring his trains on our trips. I realized that he was using the trains for comfort and a safety net. For him, the trains represented certainty. Even though we were out on trips, the trains helped him feel grounded and "at home." Once I understood why my son needed his trains on our trips, I did not react the same way. Instead, I helped him find a way to better carry them. As he got older, he didn't need to bring his trains on trips. Now, he is doing well in school and adjusting to life. I'm so proud of my son!

> *"Self-esteem is the experience of being competent to cope with the basic challenges of life and being worthy of happiness."*
> Nathaniel Branden

As you become more self-aware, you'll be able to manage your thoughts, emotions and behaviors. Ultimately, your life will be improved as you know yourself and accept yourself more! Now, let's discuss some of the benefits of being self-aware.

The Benefits of Being Self-Aware

All of the benefits of being self-aware are too enormous to list. However, I want to outline just a few. In my observations as a psychotherapist, I discovered that self-aware people are often spiritually, psychologically and physically centered. They have learned the secret to a healthy and a balanced lifestyle. This means they have learned to be happy and enjoy everyday life. While they are aware of the chaos of life, they focus on the positive aspects of it. They choose to focus on what they can change rather than complain about what they cannot change. They are committed to ongoing learning.

When you are self-aware you will better know who you are, as well as your strengths and weaknesses. You will be better prepared to maximize your strengths and seek help for your weaknesses. Here are some of the core benefits you can expect to enjoy when you are self-aware:

1. **The ability to better express yourself**
When you are self-aware, you know how to effectively express yourself and communicate your thoughts,

feelings and desires. As you become more self-aware you will be more comfortable with setting proper boundaries within yourself and with others. This means that you will be in a better position to say **NO** when you mean no, and **YES** when you mean it.

2. **Higher self-esteem**

What is Self-Esteem? It is *"...a person's overall sense of self-worth. It is the experience of being competent to cope with the basic challenges of life and being worthy of happiness"* (Nathaniel Branden). Merriam-Webster defines self-esteem as "*The quality or state of having certain certitude...of being contented or satisfied.*" As your self-esteem improves, you'll become more authentic and live a more fulfilled life.

> **Self-esteem is the quality or state of having certain certitude.**

3. **Higher self-confidence**

Self-confidence is your innate perception of yourself. It is often used interchangeably with self-esteem, but they are two distinct psychological concepts. Self-esteem is the internal assessment of your worth.

Self-confidence is the belief in your ability to do something. For example, a person may have great confidence in their ability to sing and perform other artistic skills, but a low overall self-worth.

People with high self-confidence and F will often focus excessively on a particular skill, believing it will earn them respect, love and significance. I recommend that you continue to work on your self-confidence *and* self-esteem. Both are necessary toward developing a healthy personhood.

3 Tips to Improve Your Self-Awareness

The most important step toward building healthy relationships is self-awareness. In any relationship, you can only offer who you are, to improve what you have. That is why it's critical to continuously work toward building healthier relationships.

There is no secret on how to improve self-awareness. It's a process that differs with each person. But here are three steps to get you started:

- Identify your core values
- Identify and acknowledge your strengths and weaknesses
- Commit to continued growth and development

Identify Your Core Values

Core values are the things most important to you, the principles that shape your mindset, actions and results. If you have not identified your core values, use the following chart as a starting point.

The Justin's Core Values Chart

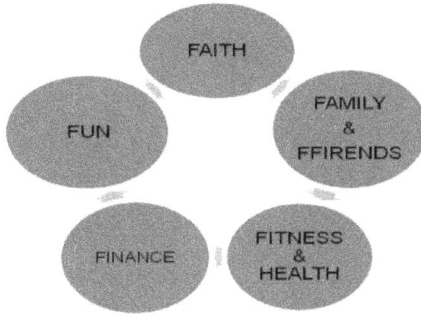

Identifying your core values will give you the following benefits:

- Fewer disappointments
- Greater self-awareness
- Focus and direction in life
- Prioritizing what matters most in *your* life
- More certainty, fulfillment and happiness

It's important to identify your core values, since they determine your actions, and your actions determine your results.

Whenever we choose to go against what we truly believe, we usually end up losing a little bit of ourselves. When faced with ethically challenging situations, always remember that your decision will impact your essence. I believe you can achieve your goals without compromising your values and your life.

Identify and Acknowledge Your Strengths and Weaknesses

Recently, everyone in my team took a basic online personality test. You've probably taken similar tests like this before, where you end up with some sort of acronym, symbol or number that categorizes you as a certain type of individual. The idea is that once you understand your specific combination of characteristics, you can use that information to improve yourself and to build healthier relationships. Also, the insight from such assessments can help you work with your peers more effectively and manage your time more efficiently.

The result of my quiz was disturbingly accurate. As usual there were certain statements that made me feel good, such as my ability to organize and accomplish tasks. However, there were qualities that made me feel embarrassed and uncomfortable. Secretly, I desired more competence with multi-tasking, as well as greater comfort in working independently. But this personality test revealed the opposite!

After some time to process the results of my personality quiz, I've developed two lessons from which we can all benefit. For instance, I'm good at:

- Researching, writing and public-speaking.
- Talking with my kids and listening to those in need to provide the best counseling possible.

- I'm also good at accepting and working on my weaknesses, such as my vision disability. I have learned to accept the reality of my limitations and overcome my obstacles, as well as the fact that I cannot change what I don't understand and accept.

We all have our weaknesses. Some of mine include:

- Keeping my life stress-free.
- Being nice when I'm too tired.
- Balancing my work life and personal life.

Since you cannot improve what you don't identify and understand, one of the best ways to identify your strengths and weaknesses is to—as I did—write down three things you are good at, and three qualities you want to improve upon. If you are unable to come up with a list, ask the people most familiar with you for help. You can also take a personality test.

This exercise will help you get started in your process of identifying and acknowledging your strengths and weaknesses. Once identified, you can get a life coach or a mentor to help you overcome the obstacles preventing your success and happiness, and develop a plan to maximize your strengths. As a professional coach I would love to help you in this process. Feel free to email me by visiting CoachJamesJustin.com.

Commit to Continued Growth and Development

Self-awareness is a process. The process is different for each person. You'll continue to evolve as you discover and understand more information about yourself. That is why it's important to commit to continued growth and development. As you commit to higher self-awareness and take actions toward your goals, you'll achieve greater success, joy and happiness!

Step 1 Summary

Self-awareness is about knowing who you are. It's a lifetime process of learning, accepting and improving who you are. It requires patience and persistence. It is the initial step to develop healthy relationships with anyone you desire. In any relationship, you can only offer who you are and what you have. Therefore, it is necessary to take the time to get to know yourself. If you do not know who you are, how can you know what you really want in a relationship?

When you who you are, you are more confident in developing healthy relationships. **Step 1** highlighted the major factors that influence self-Awareness. It covered the following concepts:

- The meaning of self-awareness
- The benefits of self-awareness
- 3 tips to improve your self-awareness

If you want to learn more about self-awareness in creating the relationships you desire, I encourage you to read and apply what you have learned from this book.

Step 2

Become Selective

Who do you want to be your **PALs**? In pursuing healthy relationships, it's important to acknowledge who is best suited to be in your circle of influence. Your **PALs** can make or break you.

> *"A friend to all is a friend to none."*
> Aristotle

Since a friend to everyone is a friend to none, it is essential for you to become selective. The goal of this step is to help you to become wiser in selecting the right people to develop healthy relationships with. You'll learn what I mean by being "selective." More importantly, you'll be introduced to Justin's **PAL** circles and the **CARD** concept as tools to assist you in selecting the right people to develop healthy relationship with.

You will become like the company you keep.

I define "selective" as a conscious and proactive process of choosing your relationships carefully. The selective process empowers you to choose the right

Peers, **A**ssociates and **L**oved ones (**PAL**). I encourage you to explore your *own* definition and methods of choosing your friends wisely, for you will become like the company you keep. Since you cannot develop healthy relationships with everyone, you must select the people you will allow to enter your inner circle.

Deciding who to allow into your inner circle is made simple with the knowledge that the company you keep will determine your level of success or failure. I like J. Willard Marriott's interpretation of this concept: *"Choose your friends wisely—they will make or break you."*

Since you can't please everyone, it is impossible to develop healthy relationships with everyone. For instance, some people just will not like me for any particular or specific reason. The same is true for you. My opinion is that one third of people will like you, one third will dislike you and the other third are undecided. Thus, one out of three people will like you. Instead of wasting your precious time and energy on people who do not like you, invest your resources in developing healthy relationships with those who do. Trying to please everyone is self-defeating and will serve only to make you miserable.

| **Choose your friends wisely, for you will become like the company you keep.**

Personal experience and research has taught me to be selective in developing new relationships with those who are capable, available, reliable and dependable. This applies to making friends, choosing a soul mate and developing new associates.

As a counselor and business owner, I work with different types of people. I learned many lessons from dealing with people including the fact that most people are driven by their emotions rather than their capacity for reason. I also learned that there are some people who do not want to change, but want to remain "professional complainers." In the past I wanted to *please* everyone because I wanted to be *friends* with everyone. However, in the process of realizing that I cannot please everyone, I finally found peace in my acceptance of that fact. My life is better without these folks. Armed with that knowledge, I am much happier. In fact, I am now known as "that happiness guy" among my friends and clients.

> **I choose to be in the company of those who will love me, accept me and challenge me to grow.**

Who do you need to let go in order to create room for the right people to come in your life? Once you identify the people you want to let go, take immediate action. The more you delay, the longer it will take to attract the right people.

The more self-aware I become, the more I realize that there are some people that I need to let go of if I want to succeed in life. In my self-assessment I discovered that I am not meant to serve everyone. I am called to serve a select few who are willing to transform, optimize and accelerate their lives to greater success, joy and happiness. My current focus is on those who God calls me to serve and those who are willing to work with me. I am happier and more productive with that realization, and I hope the same for you.

I choose my friends wisely because I learned that the company I keep determines my level of success. My environment plays an important role on what I think, feel and do. "Do not be misled: "Bad company corrupts good character" *(1 Corinthians 15:33)*. If I want to develop healthy relationships, I must interact regularly with those who share similar mindsets. Since I want to be successful, I choose to select my friends and other associates wisely. I choose to be in the company of those who will love me, accept me and challenge me to grow.

The decision to select my relationships wisely was a process. In my younger years I tried to be friends with many to no avail. I gave my time, energy and guidance. However, when I was in need, those "friends" were nowhere to be found. I eventually I learned my lesson on the importance of being selective. I discovered that it's imperative to have a guideline for selecting the right people to develop healthy relationship with. Consequently, I developed the Justin's **PAL** Circles as a tool to categorize my relationships.

The Justin's PAL Circles

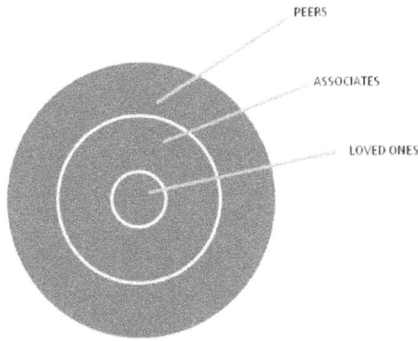

A pal is a friend. However, since there are different levels of friendship, I divide my friends into three groups based on the level of intimacy. This tool helps me set proper boundaries and expectations with my friends. My levels of friendship are as follows:

Peers
My peers include any fellow human beings—people with a similar knowledge base, abilities, skills, qualifications, age and background. I believe we are all equal in the journey of life. We all have something to teach and to share with each other.

Associates
My associates include my partners or colleagues in business or at work.

Loved ones
This group includes my nuclear and extended family members and close friends.

How do you decide who enters your **PAL** circles? Your **PAL**s are the people you regard as your friends, the people in your circle of influence. Take time to select the right people to be in your circles because they'll impact your life.

The **CARD** concept is another tool I use to select the right people in my circles of influence. You're welcome to adopt and explore this tool as a practical guide in selecting your friends. It reveals certain qualities that you should expect from your friends.

You can start the process of deciding what qualities you desire in your **PAL**s by writing a list of characteristics of a healthy relationship that are important to you. For example, my oldest son already began the process of deciding what kind of girl he wants to befriend. He decided that he wants to explore friendships with those who are "smart and pretty." These are the qualities that are important to my ten-year-old son. If he can begin the selective process at age 10, he will improve on his method of selection as an adult. I am sure that most adults can create a thorough list of qualities they want in a friend. Now, let's explore the theory behind **CARD**.

Compatible
Compatibility is the state or quality of existing together in harmony, love and respect. In healthy relationships each party must be compatible or at least willing to work in harmony toward compatibility. This may include adapting similar mindsets, core values and hobbies. For example, when my wife and I met, we were not

compatible. She was already in college and I was finishing my secondary education. Our parents did not believe we were a good match. However, we decided to work on ourselves individually together. Today, we are best friends.

Available

Availability is the state or quality of being accessible to your friends, and being available when needed. I subscribe to the philosophy behind the Haitian proverb that reads, *"You can tell who your friends are when you are in need."* It is easy to be available to someone when there is no need. However, it takes a healthy friend to care for you when you are in need. Availability is one of the characteristics to look for when choosing friends and healthy relationships. We are more likely to develop bonds and do business with people who are readily available. We are comfortable with people we know. I am more likely to develop healthy friendships with a group of individuals I interact with frequently, and who are willing to be my friends. Practically, healthy friendships usually share the same church, school, work and proximity. Other avenues through which to explore meeting potential friends include the following:

- Local churches
- The YMCA or gym
- Civic and community groups
- Local Chambers of Commerce
- Local libraries and book clubs
- School Parent/Teacher Organizations

- Parties and local social gatherings
- Social media websites

While these are great settings to meet people on a regular basis, developing and nurturing healthy relationships is only possible when we leave our "comfort zones" in an effort to develop healthy friendships. Availability alone is not enough to build healthy friendships.

In life, few things happen by chance. If you want to pursue healthy friendships, you must work at it and apply the **CARD** principles as you begin the process. For example, I worked for seven years with a group of people, but only developed a basic level of friendship. We had the opportunity to progress the relationship from the "peer" level to the "loved ones" level, but did not take advantage of it. Perhaps it was because we did not extend the interactions beyond work, did not share commonalities and were not in the same thought vibrations. Therefore, the relationships did not last when my employment ended.

Nevertheless, I learned valuable lessons from that experience. I learned that I was not aware of the seven steps to healthy relationships. I did not know how to effectively develop such relationships outside the circle of my family and close friends. I have since adopted the seven steps to work toward setting proper boundaries in relationships, as well as the importance of ongoing communications in developing healthy relationships.

The communication efforts, though, must be reciprocal and mutually beneficial

Respectable
Respectability is a state of being admired by your friends. It requires a positive attitude, and holds a person in high honor or esteem. Respect is a mutual behavior, and provides a productive environment to grow friendships.

Driven
Drive is an attitude and motivation to achieve desires. I have found that people who are driven are more likely to encourage and support others around them to do the same. You can decide whether you need a friend who is not driven or motivated to achieve anything in life. But as an achiever, I thrive on being in the company of people who are motivated and driven to pursue their life purpose.

The **CARD** acronym provides a brief list of friendship qualities. My goal is to encourage you to create your own list by giving you a head start. Friendship is such an important part of life. We were created to interact and socialize with others. We need to cooperate with healthy people to achieve our callings. Therefore, I urge you to reflect on the characteristics of your friendships in an effort to plan and pursue friendships with those who share your core values, and who at least meet the **CARD** qualities.

Step 2 Summary

The best way to summarize this step is through the following quotes:

"Choose your relationships wisely, for your success depends on it."

James Justin

"Be careful the environment you choose, for it will shape you; be careful the friends you choose, for you will become like them."

W. Clement Stone

"Don't make friends who are comfortable to be with. Make friends who will force you to lever yourself up."

Thomas J. Watson

"You can make more friends in two months by becoming genuinely interested in other people, than you can in two years by trying to get other people interested in you."

Dale Carnegie

Step 3

Become the Friend You Want to Attract

"If you go looking for a friend, you're going to find they're very scarce. If you go out to be a friend, you'll find them everywhere."

Zig Ziglar

We all know that friendship is important in life. But did you know that friends have a major impact on your success, happiness and quality of life? There are many benefits you will enjoy when you have great friends. They are a great source of love and support. They can help you achieve your goals, and comfort you when you feel lonely, isolated and depressed. But despite the benefits of friendship, great friends don't "just happen."

The reality is that many of us struggle to meet new friends and develop healthy relationships. Even when willing to invest the time and effort to acquire these healthy relationships, we don't always know how to go about it.

It's never too late to develop new friends or reconnect with old ones. The process can be fun and fulfilling. To help you build healthier friendships, you'll learn the following:

- How to recognize your true friends and what to look for in a friend
- The benefits of friendship
- Why making new friends can be challenging
- 3 tips to boost your friendliness skills
- 7 tips for making new friends

How to Recognize Your True Friends, and What to Look for in a Friend

In your search for new friends to build healthy relationships, it's important to recognize who is truly a friend to you. Here are some definitions to get started:

- A friend is someone you trust, and shares a deep level of understanding and connection with you.

- A friend is someone who is truthful with you, and will help nurture your growth, development and full potential.

- A friend is someone you like; shares your values, interest and mindset; and someone you enjoy being with.

Social media technology is a new factor affecting how we define friendship. Presently, a "friend" is a click away. Using social media sites such as Facebook, Twitter and LinkedIn, we can instantly add a new friend to our online friendship list. We can also reconnect with old friends fairly quickly. However, having hundreds of online friends is not the same as having great friends you can turn to or be with in person.

I appreciate technology and encourage you to explore social media as a viable tool and component in developing healthy friendships. For example, it makes it convenient to keep in touch with current friends. It also facilitates social opportunities to reconnect with old friends and spark new connections with people around the world who share your interests.

Online connections toward building healthy friendships are limited, though. Your online friends can't hug you when you need it the most. They can't visit you when you're in the hospital, or celebrate a happy occasion with you. I believe our most important connections happen when we're face-to-face. There's no technology that can replace direct human contact. So, make it a priority to stay in touch in the "real" world, not just virtually. The key is to combine technology and face-to-face dialogue in order to develop healthy relationships with anyone you so desire.

When seeking new friends, there are many characteristics to look for. Ultimately, you'll have to decide what's important to you. In **Step 2** you were introduced to the Justin's **PAL** circles, and the **CARD** concept, which you can use as guidelines to develop healthy relationships. They are tools I use to select *my* friends and those in my circles of influence. You can use these tools as a starting point for choosing *your* new friends as well.

When seeking new friends, don't focus solely on the external qualifications, ignoring the internal beauty of the person. The most important component in healthy friendship is how the relationship makes you feel; not how it looks on paper, how many things you have in common or what others think. I recommend that you focus on both the external *and* internal qualities of potential friends.

In an effort to discern whether someone has true potential toward a healthy friendship, ask yourself the following questions:

- Do I feel better after spending time with this person?

- Do I feel free to be myself around this person?

- Do I feel safe, or do I feel like I am walking on egg shells with this person?

- Is the person supportive of me? Do they treat me with respect and equality?

- Is this a person I feel that I can trust?

The bottom line is that if the friendship *feels* great, it *is* great. However, if you feel unhappy and believe that the relationship will go nowhere, you owe it to yourself to move on. I recommend that you stay away from unhealthy relationships with anyone. An unhealthy relationship is poison to your spirit, soul and body.

What are the qualities you want your friends to have? Let's get started! Start this process by writing a list of characteristics that you value in relationship. Next, take some time to find people who share your values, interests and mindset.

It's time for YOU to develop healthier relationships. Let go unhealthy relationships and take some risk to develop new friends!

| **To grow, you must take risks.** |

To develop healthier friendship, take some calculated risk. I believe that you'll have great friends as you continue to apply the steps outlined in this book.

The Benefits of Friendship

> *"I cannot even imagine where I would be today were it not for that handful of friends who have given me a heart full of joy. Let's face it; friends make life much more fun."*
> Charles R. Swindoll

Great friends add special meaning to life. They help you share the good times and the bad times. Among other things, good friends can:

- **Improve your mood.** Happiness can be infectious. Spending time with happy and positive friends can elevate your mood and boost your outlook.

- **Help you to reach your goals.** Whether you're trying to get fit, give up smoking or otherwise improve your life, encouragement from a friend can really boost your willpower and increase your chances of success.

- **Reduce your stress and depression.** Having an active social life can bolster your immune system and help reduce isolation, a major contributing factor for depression.

- **Support you through tough times.** Even if it's just having someone to share your problems with, friends can help you cope with serious illness, the loss of a job or loved one, the breakup of a relationship or any other challenge in life.

- **Support you as you age.** As you age, retirement, illness, and the death of loved ones can often leave you isolated. Having people, you can turn to for company and support can provide purpose as you age, and be a buffer against depression, disability, hardship, and loss. Staying socially engaged as you age keeps you feeling positive and boosts your happiness.

- **Heighten your sense of self-worth.** Friendship is a two-way street, and the "give" side of the give-and-take contributes to your own sense of value and self-worth. Being there for your friends makes you feel needed and adds purpose to your life.

Why Making New Friends Can Be Challenging

There are many reasons it's difficult to make new friends. The major one is fear. Fear can manifest in various forms. The most common one is fear of rejection.

Making new friends can be risky, but the reward is greater. To grow, you must take risks. To succeed, you need a team; a group of friends who can help you achieve your goals.

However, making new friends does not have to be *too* risky. You can minimize your risk by taking your time and develop your best method in meeting new people. For example, you can get potential friendship referrals from current or old friends. I know you'll be putting yourself out there to meet new people. However, you can do it selectively. Review **Step 2** of this book for tips on how to select your friends wisely. These tips will empower you to overcome the fear of rejection.

3 Tips to Boost Your Friendliness Skills

Friendliness is a choice. It's a skill that can be developed with practice. You can *choose* to be friendly to everyone you meet. Just because you are friendly does not mean you must be friends with everyone. However, if you want people to treat you kindly and in a friendly matter, you must first practice it. Here are three tips to boost your friendliness skills:

1. **Learn to Smile**
   A warm smile is the universal language of friendliness. When you smile, you shine. When you meet new people or see people you know, please smile at them. As Mother Teresa once said, *"Peace begins with a smile."* A smile is also contagious. Generally, if you smile at people they are more likely to return the smile. When smiling, look in the direction of the people to whom you are smiling. Practice your smile while looking in the mirror. In the words of Maya Angelou: *"If you have only one smile in you, give it to the people you love."*

2. **Learn to Be Yourself**
   There is nothing more repelling than being someone you are not. You may be able to fool people sometimes, but the truth is soon revealed. Eventually, people will discover who you truly are. Therefore, I urge you to be yourself by being authentic and avoiding "fake self."

I've tried to be like others to no avail. Now, I strive to be who God made me to be. I simply accept who I am, and I find it easier to make new friends. I am happier now that I accept myself.

> *"A friend is someone who gives you total freedom to be yourself."*
>
> Jim Morrison

If you want to attract healthy friendships, it is important to learn to accept just being yourself. The more you try to be some you're not, the more you will repel people from you. If you want to have healthy friendships, you must learn how to influence others and attract them to you. As you become self-aware, self-confident and self-accepting, you will be more effective in attracting the right friends.

Again, I highly recommend that you become self-aware and accept who you are. You cannot accept others unless you have accepted yourself. When you are self-aware, you will be able to address your issues effectively, and maximize your strengths to attract the right friends.

Whatsoever you practice in secret will be revealed in public.

You will be able to express yourself with ease, and better able to communicate with others. Before you pursue healthy friendships, utilize your self-awareness and address your issues "back stage" with those who love you. Your friends will be more receptive to help you address your issues and maximize your abilities. If you do not manage your issues effectively in private, they may show up on stage when you least expect it.

3. **Learn to Love Others as Yourself**
   "Greater love has no one than this, than to lay down one's life for his friends" *(John 15:13)*. If you love yourself, love God and love others, you will never be without friends, for everyone is looking to be friends with loving people.

Now that you have some friendly tools, it is time to take some practical steps on your journey to make new friends.

7 Tips to Make New Friends

Great friends are developed over time. If you want great friends, you must *become* the friend you want to find, since we often attract who we are. As Michael Losier says it: *"I attract to my life whatever I give my attention, energy and focus to, whether positive or negative."* In addition to having the mindset and quality to attract the friends you want, you need to take action and go to local places where you can meet people.

To make new friends, you need a circle where you can meet potential people on a regular basis. The following tips will be your guide:

1. **Talk to Your Neighbors**
   It is surprising to me how many people do not know their next-door neighbors. And it is not necessarily your fault, but the consequence of our busy American culture. After a long day at work you just want to get home and relax. But before you close the garage door be sure to say hello to the person living right next to you that you might see coming home at the same time. Do something nice for them, like helping them with groceries or even giving them a small plant as a "hello neighbor" type of gift. Slowly get to know them and you may become friends. Even if you don't become friends, get some practice for the next people you will meet at work or elsewhere.

2. **Get Out of Your Home or Apartment**
   Instead of logging on at home, take your e-reader device or laptop out to the coffee shop occasionally. It may be an opportunity to meet great people. Remember, whatsoever you seek, you will find. If you seek friends, you will find them if you get out of your comfort zone. Just by being "out," you will be able to meet more people than you will by staying at home all the time. You can meet in other settings such as a local church, dry cleaner, mall or coffee shop. When you visit the same store every week, it will help the staff and other patrons recognize you. This helps you connect when you see those same people again elsewhere. The main key is to *get out* and find the friends your heart desires.

3. **Get a Part-Time Job**
   The workplace is a great setting to meet people on a regular basis. If you are desperately looking for new friends and you have tried other methods, consider getting a part-time job. You will not only meet the people working with you, but if you choose wisely you will also get a chance to meet customers. In fact, one of my former employees found her husband while on the job; he was one of our clients.

4. **Ditch the Drive-Thru**
   Go inside the restaurant to place your order. You may find people to chat with. And don't be in a rush. That is the only way this method can be

effective. For if your mind is elsewhere you will not have the patience to make small talk with potential friends.

5. **Attend Networking Events**
   Going to events and local activities is one way to meet people and make new friends. However, it is an activity that some people avoid due to fear and lack of confidence. I used to be like that. I avoided many network marketing events because of irrational fears. However, I confronted my fear of meeting new people. My experience reveals that most fears are irrational. They are **F**alse **E**vidence **A**ppearing **R**eal (**FEAR**). There is usually no spiritual or scientific basis for most fears. I believe that most of what we fear never manifests, and that some can be "repaired" with minimal consequence or fees.

   To help me with the fear of networking, I took an etiquette business class. The class equipped me with the tools required for effective networking in business and social situations. The class facilitator was Barbara Bergstrom, author of "Bound for the Boardroom: Learn Today How You Can Know the Difference to Make a Difference." In addition to completing the coaching class, I invested time, energy, money and meditation on self-development. I learned to become independent, yet dependent upon God and others. This is one of the benefits of being self-aware: the ability to accept one's strengths and humanity.

6. **Practice Small Talk When Meeting New People**
One way I practice small talk is to do it with current friends or a family member when I don't have to. When I walk in a place of business I greet people with a smile. But that is fine because I still get some practice. It used to be difficult for me to initiate small talk with strangers, but it is much easier now that I am more confident. I know it can be intimidating to engage in small talk, but it can be a very rewarding opportunity to meet a potential friend, partner or client. Here are some suggestions that made me more comfortable making small talk with others:

- **Keep it light.** Use light and positive topics during your small talk conversations. You can draw on topics such as weather, comedy shows, music, shopping, current TV shows and sports.

- **Think positive.** It is difficult to initiate conversation with new people. But having a positive mindset will produce positive outcomes. If you adopt a positive mindset, you will attract like-minded people. If you get anxious when meeting new people, you are not alone. It is okay. Many of us have experienced anxiety when meeting new people. However, it gets easier with practice and by adopting a positive mindset. Positive thinking is a great way for us to overcome this type of anxiety. It helps us to focus on the desired outcome. For example, I learned to focus on the fun I will have at a party, rather than obsessing on the fact that I will not know anyone there. Rather than focusing on becoming tongue-tied during small talk, picture yourself chatting away with your best friends. Positive thinking has been shown to aid in stress management, which can help you conquer your anxiety of meeting new people. When you think positive you will often attract positive thinkers, which makes it easier to initiate small talk.

- **Keep practicing.** As you continue to learn new information on small talk, practice it! Start by reading online articles on the subject including "The Fine Art of Small Talk" by Debra Fine.

7. **Connect Through the Process of Rapport Building**
Rapport is a term derived from the French word rapporteur (reporter), which means to bring back a message. It is the process of building trust and

respect, characterized by a harmonious and mutual relationship. Proper rapport takes place when two or more people are in sync, or on the same thought vibration or wavelength because they feel similar and relate well to each other. Why is proper rapport so important, and how can it be used to develop healthy friendships?

- **Utilize rapport.** Generally, people become friends with those they like and those they have proper rapport with. People are more receptive to engage in friendships with people similar to themselves. It is a universal law of attraction. It helps us attract those with similar mindsets and emotional quotients. When this law is well understood it can be used to build proper rapport. For example, I can tell within minutes if an interviewee is in rapport with me by watching how they mirror and reciprocate my body language, as well as other nonverbal cues.
In everyday life, building rapport can help with persuasion, sales, marketing, teamwork, dating, loving and, of course, healthy relationships. Remember, proper rapport is established when two or more people are harmoniously in sync and can express it through the process of mirroring and reciprocating each other's nonverbal cues.

- **Mirroring body language.** When we are connected with people, we tend to mirror their posture and body movements. It is a natural process that takes place subconsciously. We may not be aware that we are mirroring, even if we are professionally trained. If you want to practice mirroring, wait 10 seconds and then shift your body in the same way as the person you are currently with.

  This is important because people do business with people they like. Therefore, if you want to be friends with certain people, you want to improve your likeability scale to theirs. You can achieve this goal with necessary time, mirroring and reciprocating their body language. Yes, it takes time to develop healthy friendships. According to Dr. Lauretta Justin, *"Nothing in life happens by osmosis."* Therefore, I urge you to be patient in developing proper rapport with people.

- **Commonality.** Commonality is a process of finding something in common with a person or a customer in an effort to build a sense of camaraderie and trust. This is very important because it is required to develop healthy friendships. Remember, people often pursue friendships with those who share interests, values, likes, dislikes and other commonalities.

- **Reciprocity.** This is another way to build rapport with others. It can be done in many ways such as gifts and spending time and money to reciprocate a behavior. Whatever method you use to reciprocate friendly gestures, be sure that it is done out of love rather than "paying back" a friend. The key is the *motive* for the gift. If it is not based on love, re-think your motivation.

Remember, it takes time and effort to develop healthy friendships. Don't rush the process. Let new friendships develop slowly. Sometimes the easiest way to make friends is to be informal about it. You do not have to be pushy; you just need to be patient. As you meet people every day, let the relationship develop at its own natural pace.

You must be selective, since you cannot be friends with everyone. However, you *can* take your time to get to know the people you meet. You may connect faster with certain people who share your interests than with others, and that is perfectly normal. Keep a positive attitude as you meet new people, and set proper expectations and boundaries so that you do not get disappointed. In the event you get disappointed, you can always try again with someone else who is willing to be your friend.

> *"Truly great friends are hard to find, difficult to leave, and impossible to forget."*
>
> Unknown

Eventually, some of the folks you meet on a casual basis will become your friends, and a few may become healthy friendships. It is my firm belief that you will make as many friends as your heart desires if you apply the principles in this book. These principles have changed *my* relationships, and I pray for the same outcomes for you. As your coach I encourage you to invest time in healthy relationships with friends who will help you achieve your life purpose, as you help them as well. I believe that you will be able to connect with others more effectively as you continue to practice the principles outlined in this chapter.

Step 3 Summary

If you want a friend, you must first become one. Developing great friends is a process, but the rewards are enormous. Good friends are a great source of comfort, love and support. They can help you when you feel lonely, isolated and depressed. Your friends can also help you achieve your goals. As you continue to practice the principles provided in this step, you'll be able to make new friends more confidently, and improve your relationship with current friends!

Step 4

Become an Effective Communicator

> *"To effectively communicate, we must realize that we are all different in the way we perceive the world, and use this understanding as a guide to our communication with others"*
>
> Anthony Robbins

The building block for any relationship is communication. Communication is a skill that can be developed over time with coaching and directed effort.

In order to develop healthy relationships, we must first understand how to communicate effectively. There are many people who can talk, but few know how to *communicate* effectively.

Listening is only one of the keys to effective communication. There are other tools you must add to your tool kit to become an effective communicator.

This step is an introductory course on effective communication. It offers practical tips you can use to improve your communication skills in your effort to develop healthy relationship with anyone you so desire. You'll learn the following concepts:

- The meaning of effective communication
- Verbal and nonverbal communication
- 3 Obstacles preventing effective communication
- The **SLOW** communication acronym
- The benefits of effective communication in healthy relationship

What is Effective Communication?

Effective communication is an ongoing process that takes time and effort. If you are willing to learn and *apply* what you have discovered, you will become an effective communicator. The tools provided in this step will empower you to achieve that goal. Let's first define communication.

| **Effective communication is a beautiful art when used in the context of love and mutuality.**

Julia Wood, the author of "Communication Mosaics" defines communication as "A *systemic process in which people interact with and through symbols to create and interpret meanings.*" Note the word "process." This means that one must undergo gradual changes that lead to a particular result. In this case, the result is effective communication.

In order to develop healthy relationships there must be a process of communication. When the process of communication is working, there is an authentic rapport and dialogue. In that process there are verbal and nonverbal methods of exchanging symbols, signs, behaviors and words between the parties involved. As a result, the messages are clear, and each party can interpret the meaning of the messages. This process of communication builds commonalities, which continuously fortify healthy relationships. Once developed, effective communication is a beautiful art when used in the context of love and mutuality.

Verbal and Nonverbal Communication

In counseling school, I discovered the concepts of verbal and nonverbal communication. Verbal communication refers to our spoken words that express our thoughts, feelings and behaviors. This excludes written expressions. Whereas, nonverbal communication refers to gestures, facial expressions and any body language that does not involve written or verbal communication. This process includes body posture, accent, tone of voice and eye contact.

Nonverbal communication actually speaks *louder* than verbal communication. I believe that effective communication is 80 percent nonverbal and only 20 percent verbal. As so insightfully stated by Jim Rohn, "*Effective communication is 20 percent what you know, and 80 percent how you* feel *about what you know.*" The percentage of verbal and nonverbal communication can be broken down further.

Here is what Professor Albert Mehrabian's communication research revealed:

- 7 percent of the message pertaining to feelings and attitudes is in the words that are spoken.
- 38 percent of the message pertaining to feelings and attitudes is paralinguistic—the way that the words are said.

- 55 percent of the message pertaining to feelings and attitudes is in facial expression (businessballs.com).

When you are engaged in communication with people, it's critical to pay attention to your verbal and nonverbal clues, since both forms of communication will impact your message.

3 Obstacles Preventing Effective Communication

There are many obstacles that can block communication. As you learn how to communicate effectively, you'll discover how to manage and eliminate the obstacles preventing your success. I recommend that you create a list of obstacles that block your communication flow, and develop a plan of action to overcome them.

Here are three obstacles to get you started:

1. **Fatigue**
   This can be a major obstacle blocking effective communication. Fatigue is physical or mental exhaustion that can be triggered by stress, overwork and lack of adequate sleep. When I am tired it's harder for me to express myself effectively and listen attentively. I find it very difficult to focus when I am tired. I usually, postpone important conversations with my loved ones and clients until I am rested. Since it is important for me to pay attention to my family, friends and others, I avoid important dialogues until I am fully rested and able to communicate effectively.

2. **A vague message**
   A speaker's message must be succinct and lucid. If not, the listener is left to interpret the message without fully understanding the speaker's intent. If you want to become an effective communicator, I encourage you to first identify your message and speak it with enthusiasm in the language that your listeners can best understand. This process will help captivate the attention of your listeners, and your message will be perceived with clarity and intention.

3. **Lack of interest in the topic**
   From my experience as a speaker, teacher and counselor, I have observed that a lack of interest

on the topic at large makes it difficult to communicate effectively. We only pay attention to what we value. To become an effective communicator, you must develop an interest in the conversation. You must engage your audience. To achieve that goal, simply ask questions about your listeners' interests.

In order to establish and maintain effective communication in healthy relationships, all involved parties must agree to consistent communication. This allows each party an equal opportunity to share their thoughts, feelings, and ideas toward building healthy relationships. Through effective communication, each member is able to express themselves openly.

The S.L.O.W Communication Concept

I utilize the **S.L.O.W** communication concept which stands for (**S**peaking, **L**istening, **O**bserving and **W**aiting) patiently to help me improve my communication skills. Feel free to use it as a starting point to master effective communication.

Speaking
As an effective communicator, it is important to continuously develop your speaking skills. Before you speak be certain that you have something worth saying, and that your message is *clear and concise*. When communicating, it is imperative to be mindful of the listener and to protect the conversation from the

communication killers. The human mind can be easily distracted by external and internal stimuli. Externally it may include background noise from the surrounding environment. Internal distractions include clutter and a host of other pre-occupations and inner conflicts, thoughts and emotions. Thus, it is imperative to first capture the attention of your audience by making the message clear, concise and exciting. A vague message leads to vague interpretation.

Listening

I recommend that you listen twice before speaking. Also consider the carpenter's rule: "Measure twice—cut once." King Salomon stated it this way: "He who answers a matter before he hears it, it is folly and shame to him" (*Proverbs 18:13*). There is a reason we have two ears and only one mouth. Perhaps God wants us to listen twice before we speak. In my experience the wise listens before speaking, whereas, the fool never stops talking. God created us with a natural ability to hear. However, *listening* is a skill that must be developed with patience and persistence.

> **There is a reason we have two ears and only one mouth. Perhaps God wants us to listen twice before we speak.**

In order to establish effective communication, you must possess critical listening skills. Critical listening is a state or quality of listening attentively.

When listening, pay close attention to what is said by the speaker and what is *not* being said. This process enables you to learn about the speaker's full intent. In psychology, we called this process "active listening."

Active listening is a communication technique often used in counseling, life coaching and conflict resolution. It's a technique where the listener gives feedback to the speaker to ensure that they are on the same page and understand the message of the speaker. As professional listeners we practice active listening by re-stating or paraphrasing, eye contact and using various body language techniques to demonstrate that we are listening.

To assess and improve your listening skills, I recommend the following:

- Complete the Justin's Listening Scale in the notes section of this book.
- Enlist the help of a life coach.
- Request a complimentary coaching session by visiting CoachJamesJustin.com.

As with other aspects of communication, listening skills can be improved as you continue to work at it.

Observing
When it comes to effective communication, it is important to be a proactive observer by taking notes and showing interest in what the speaker is saying.

This is a great way to pick up nonverbal cues from a speaker. This can be achieved at the very least by making eye contact and writing down key concepts from the speaker's message.

Waiting

Waiting is a virtue of patience. The willingness to wait for your turn to speak demonstrates maturity and respect for a speaker. This last step of the **SLOW** communication concept is vital for maintaining effective dialogue. As you wait in attentive silence, you will be able to grasp the essence of the message with more clarity. This bolsters your capacity for enlightened response and to ask relevant questions. Review and practice the **S.L.O.W** communication concept and you'll see some improvement in your communication skills. As you improve your communication skills, you'll be able to employ them in your relationships.

The Benefits of Effective Communication in Healthy Relationships

Effective communication has enormous benefits in developing healthy relationships. Communication skills are beneficial at home and in business. For example, two years ago John and Tammy came to my office seeking coaching to save their marriage. When we started working they were on the brink of a divorce. Coaching was their last effort to save their marriage. The couple loves each other, and they wanted to do everything possible to stay together. They had been married for over 20 years and raised two children. However, when their two children left home for college they found it difficult to communicate, and their marital problems worsened.

I immediately realized their problem. They had forgotten how to communicate effectively. John worked for a global company as an engineer, which entailed extensive travel. When John came home he was exhausted. He missed several of the family activities. John stated that he enjoyed his job, but he was afraid he would lose his family because of it. He realized that he had to make a choice. That's when he agreed to seek coaching.

On the other hand, Tammy had an online business selling cookware. She loved her business and was great at it. This business allowed her to stay home raising two kids while managing her profitable business.

Within three months of coaching, I was able to help John and Tammy turn their marriage around. I helped them develop a smart plan to improve their communication skills and save their marriage. They are now happier in life and in their marriage. They own several businesses together. They are copreneurs— couples in life and in business! To learn more about our clients' success stories, visit CoachJamesJustin.com and request a copy of our New Beginning program. It will inspire you and motivate you to pursue greater success, joy and happiness!

> **To become an effective communicator, you must develop an interest in the conversation.**

In addition, my wife and I experienced substantial increase in our businesses once we improved our communication with our team. When we give clear and concise instructions the team is more engaged. More importantly, our team performance doubles. Likewise, as you improve your communication skills you'll be able to more effectively express yourself at home and in your professional life.

In healthy relationships it is important to communicate openly because it builds intimacy. Even in the case of a potential friendship situation, it is advisable to communicate your thoughts and feelings within the boundaries of respect, love and wisdom. When communicating with an open mind, you will learn more from the conversation.

In healthy relationships most miscommunication can be averted if both the listener and the speaker are inclined to be open, flexible and willing to address the interferences. Both parties must agree to create a smart plan to improve their communication. John and Tammy were willing to improve their communication skills. Subsequently, they transformed their lives and their marriage. I believe that you can create similar results as you continue to improve your communication skills and create healthy relationships with those in your life. Communicating effectively with your **PALs** allows you to develop mutually beneficial relationships.

Effective communication is an ongoing process. As with a muscle, the more you use it the better you will become. Apply these concepts and tools in your daily interactions to improve your relationships. As you continue to practice these skills, you will become a better communicator.

Again, communication is a key component to establishing and maintaining any relationship. Through effective communication, narrative and personal stories are shared, advice is given and memories are made. Effective communication enables individuals to self-disclose information. It emboldens you to open up to your friends, and disclose personal information and secrets. Self-disclosure allows individuals to trust each other. The more your peers, your associates and your loved ones trust you, the more they will share their life with you. Sharing honest thoughts and feeling are important in developing healthy relationships.

Step 4 Summary

Healthy relationships contribute to a fulfilled and enlightened existence. We all want to be valued, loved, heard and cherished. However, there are few people who are willing to develop the communication skills required to promote such relationships. If you want to develop healthy relationships, you must become an effective communicator. In this step you were introduced to the following concepts:

- The meaning of effective communication
- Verbal and nonverbal communication
- 3 obstacles preventing effective communication
- The **S.L.O.W** communication acronym
- The benefits of effective communication in healthy relationships

I discussed the meaning of communication and its significance as a building block for all relationships. As defined by Merriam-Webster, communication is *"a process by which information is exchanged between individuals, through a common system of symbols, signs, or behavior."*

I discussed three obstacles preventing effective communication: **fatigue**, **a vague message** and **lack of interest in the topic.**

I outlined the four components of response toward effective communication: **S**peaking, **L**istening,

Observing and **Waiting** (**S.L.O.W**). The acronym reinforces the concept that effective communication is a progressive and evolving process. And although it mandates time and persistence, results are worth the effort.

I also discussed some the benefits of effective communication in developing healthy relationships. When you are an effective communicator, you will be empowered to fully express yourself in an effort toward developing healthy relationships. I want to conclude this step with a quote from one of my mentors, Jim Rohn: *"Take advantage of every opportunity to practice your communication skills so that when important occasions arise, you will have the gift, the style, the sharpness, the clarity and the emotions to affect other people."*

Step 5

Become Loving

"Let us always meet each other with a smile, for the smile is the beginning of love."

Mother Teresa

We now approach the apex of this book. And it would not be complete without a discussion on love. Why?   Because love is the cornerstone of healthy relationships. Where there is love, there is life. Let's explore the true meaning of love.

Love is the most important component in developing healthy relationships because without it, no one can develop such relationships. I have not seen a building stand without a solid foundation. Likewise, love is the essential foundation that keeps healthy relationships standing in all seasons.

Love is vital to a vibrant existence. It impacts how we think and feel about ourselves and others. It determines how we interact with each other on a daily basis. This step focuses on the application of love as a foundational tool to develop healthy relationships.

My research has revealed that the vitality of love in our relationships is so important that it has been passionately studied by some of the most brilliant minds in history including theologians, philosophers, poets and writers. These historical icons have researched, experienced and shared their meaning of love, and include among many others, Jesus Christ, King Solomon, Apostle Paul, Plato and Shakespeare to name just few.

Here are some of their quotes:

- Plato: *"At the touch of love everyone becomes a poet. Love is a serious mental disease."*

- Shakespeare: *"Love all, trust a few, do wrong to none."*

- Aristotle: *"Love is composed of a single soul inhabiting two bodies."*

- Jesus: *"Greater love has no one than this, than to lay down one's life for his friends"* (John 15:13).

   "A new commandment I give to you, that you love one another; as I have loved you, that you also love one another. By this all will know that you are My disciples, if you have love for one another" (John 13:34-35).

"For God so loved the world that He gave His only begotten Son, that whoever believes in Him should not perish but have everlasting life" (John 3:16).

Each of these historical figures provided meaningful quotes on love. However, I found that Jesus' meaning of love to be most helpful for human relationships and interactions. His meaning of love is not mere words, but is based on actions and passion for humanity. Therefore, I decided to present the contents on this step from a theological perspective. This is my way of honoring the work and life of Jesus.

I found the quotes on love from Jesus to be unique because He did not just teach on the subject, He *lived* it. He demonstrated His love for humanity by His passion, death and resurrection. The Bible declares, "But God demonstrates His own love toward us, in that while we were still sinners, Christ died for us" (*Romans 5:8*). Mel Gibson's film "The Passion of the Christ" is an insightful portrayal of Jesus' passion and love for humanity. As part of my research on this subject I looked up the word "love" and found the following definitions:

According to Merriam-Webster, love is *"a strong affection for another arising out of kinship or personal ties, maternal love for a child. It is attraction based on sexual desire, affection and tenderness felt by lovers. It is affection based on admiration, benevolence, or common interests. It is the fatherly concern of God for humankind, brotherly concern for others and a person's adoration of God."*

1. In Greek, there are four words to describe love:

- Agápe means unconditional love.
- Éros is an intimate and passionate love with sensual desire and sexual longing.
- Philia means friendship or affectionate love.
- Storgē means 'affection' in ancient and modern Greek. It is natural affection, like that felt by parents for children.

"The Four Loves" is a great book by C. S. Lewis, which explores the meaning and nature of love. It describes love from a Christian perspective through thought experiments, and examines Lewis' admission that he initially mistook the initial chapter of the book of John. It is written, "God is Love" as a simple beginning point to address the subject of love. I recommend reading this book for further enlightenment on the subject of love.

| **Mindsets play a major role on how we define and accept love.** |

If you ask a million people to define love you are likely to get different definitions. The reason for that is vast. We all have different worldviews or filters through which to understand the world. However, I believe that mindsets play a major role on how we define and accept love.

People often filter information and define their worldview based on their mindsets. After all, we *are* what we *think*. For example, if I have a positive mindset and positive life experience with love, I will define love from a positive perspective. However, if my mindset is negative, I will focus mostly on every problematic aspect of love.

My mindset not only impacts how I define love, it also affects how I relate with others. The above definitions provide a general meaning of love. However, I recommend that you define what love is to *you*. Use the stated definitions as a starting point.

Love is best expressed and enjoyed in real-life situations with our families, friends, neighbors, co-workers and others. Love is best defined by actions. Jesus' views and teachings about love surpassed the other historical figures mentioned because of His actions. He *proved* His love for humanity on the cross.

My favorite Biblical definition of love is recorded 1 Corinthians 13:4-8. Apostle Paul devoted an entire chapter on love. This book would not be complete without reflecting and discussing the meaning of love. In my opinion the "Love Chapter" provides a clearer picture of love than any other writings. It defines love from an action-based perspective. Let's take a closer look at the meaning of love from a Biblical perspective. I believe that this definition will help us understand what love is, and what love is not.

1. Love Is Patient

Patience is the process of waiting without becoming anxious or annoyed. It is the ability to endure life's challenges while maintaining the essence of life, and it is a virtue I continuously strive for. You would need as much patience as I do if you had three growing boys. I *used* to think that I was patient...until I had children. They are a great way to test my patience levels.

Patience plays an important role in developing healthy relationships. As I learn to become patient it is easier to manage and raise my children. I am less frustrated at their silliness and mess. Patience is of particular importance to me because two of my three children are diagnosed with Autism. The more impatient I get, the more agitated *they* get. They thrive on daily routine. My children's disability, coupled with my own disability is teaching me to be more patient, more flexible and to plan ahead. I also found meditation to be helpful in developing patience. As I learn to focus on my strengths and my children's abilities, I am becoming more patient. If I have the patience to look closer, I will find that silver lining. Do you see the silver lining in *your* cloudy day?

| Love is the fuel for patience. |

I am not sure of your life situations or issues. I am aware that this life consists of both pain and pleasure. We were all dealt different **CARD**s in life. Some of these **CARD**s are pleasant, and the others are painful at times. For some it is cancer at an early age. For my family, we are learning to cope with Autism and blindness, to focus on our abilities instead of our limitations. You may currently be dealing with your own battles. This is the nature of being in an imperfect world and living with imperfect people.

However, I want to encourage you to never give up. There is always hope for those who believe in a better day. I urge you to make the best you can out of your life situations by learning, praying, planning and celebrating any progress toward that better day. Remember, there may be an opportunity to become more patient in every situation of your life. Perhaps, you can develop patience through planning and flexibility.

In healthy relationships patience is very important. It helps you cooperate with others for extended periods of time. It takes a lot of patience to cooperate with others, and love is the fuel for patience. Patience will help you accept your friends, family and others just as they are. When people around you go through life changes, your patience will be used to love and support them in a calming manner. It certainly can help you reduce or eliminate unnecessary stress. The more patient you are, the better your life will be.

It takes time to become patient. But it is a *choice* we must all make every day. At times we may fail. But if we get back up we will succeed. God will help us if we ask diligently and earnestly. God is love, and love is patient. Therefore, we can go to Him when patience is needed.

2. Love is Kind

Kindness is a requirement to develop healthy relationships. It is the state or quality of love characterized by the willingness to help those who are truly in need. God's love is kind and generous. When I was helpless, He sent help my way, and He will do the same for you if you ask. He sent the right angels to help me in college. He knew that I would need help with my vision limitations. If you need God's kindness, you can ask Him. He can use a friend, family member or anyone else to shower you with His loving kindness.

3. Love Does Not Envy

If you are struggling with envy it is often a sign of lack of self-awareness, confidence and acceptance. When you know who you are and accept who you are, you don't need to envy.

You are a child of God. He loves you! He is your provider. Everything you need is available through him. Ask God for what you want and ask him to help you overcome envy and jealousy.

I encourage you to focus on developing yourself and don't entertain unproductive thoughts or habits that prevent your success. I encourage you to focus on your purpose and your goals.

4. Love Does Not Boast

Boasting is the excessive pride of one's glory in thought, in speech and in acts. Love certainly does not think and act selfishly. The Bible instructs us to avoid boastful mindsets and acts. "For I say, through the grace given to me, to everyone who is among you, not to think of himself more highly than he ought to think, but to think soberly, as God has dealt to each one a measure of faith" (*Romans 12:3*).

The deadliest sin is boastfulness, for those who possess it are unaware that they need help. "God resists the proud, but gives grace to the humble" (*James 4:6*). Love never boasts on anything, especially what cannot be delivered. Anyone who is boastful is also full of emptiness, and the Holy Spirit cannot dwell in him. God's love does not boast with self-praise. It is full of humility, mercy and grace. If you want to build healthy relationships, you must search your heart regularly, remove any boastful thoughts and avoid boastful deeds. Boastfulness is poison to any loving relationship.

5. Love is Not Proud

Pride is the state or quality of being pleased with one's achievements, skills or the accomplishments of loved ones. Like other thoughts and feelings, pride can be misused for selfish gain. For example, it can be distorted when a person uses it excessively to hurt themselves or others.

Boastfulness is poison to any loving relationship.

The state of pridefulness is best used in the context of love and wisdom. It is perfectly acceptable to give credit where it is due. However, it is unproductive when it is used for selfish arrogance. Love is not arrogant and bloated with pride. It is full of humbleness and meekness. While God detests pride, He loves His children. If you are struggling with pride and want to change, you can seek help. A friend or a family member can be used as an accountability partner to help you contain pride. If you want to develop healthy relationships, this habit must be replaced with love and humility.

6. Love Does Not Dishonor Others

Dishonor is a state of shame or disgrace. It is the condition of losing honor or reputation. Love does not disgrace. Instead, love fosters growth in people. Even in the case where it is required for reprimand, love does it with respect and honor. God's love is honorable and respectful. He created us with the power of choice, and He honors our decisions. Even though there are consequences for our choices, God blessed us with free will and the *opportunity* to choose."

> **Even in times where discipline is required, it must be done with love and respect. This is the way of love.**

God never forsakes or humiliates His children. In fact, He bore our shame and sins on the cross to pay the price for our sins, and to forgive us. Even when we disobey God, His heart is open, and His hands are open to accept us when we repent. Likewise, if we want to build healthy relationships we must be careful about how we treat our loved ones. We must treat people with love, honor and respect. Even in times where discipline is required, it must be done with love and respect. This is the way of love.

7. Love is Not Self Seeking
In our pre-marital counseling our pastor advised that my wife and I remove the word "I" from our vocabulary bank, and replace it with the word "we." I did not quite understand what he meant until several years into our marriage. I learned that the word "we" replaced my tendency of being selfish when interacting with my spouse. I learned that love always advocates for mutual interest. God's love does not demand its own way. Although we are all born sinners, if we believe that Christ died for our

sins, we are thus granted entry to heaven. I am grateful that He created a way for us to reconnect with Him through Jesus' sacrifice for humanity. "God demonstrates His own love toward us, in that while we are still sinners, Christ died for us" (*Romans 5:8*).

God's love is based on giving. He freely gave us life. "For God so loved the world that He gave His only begotten Son, that whoever believes in Him should not perish but have everlasting life" (*John 3:16*). Likewise, if we want to develop healthy relationships, we must be willing to love without selfishness. It is an ongoing process for us to love. However, as we learn to love and accept ourselves, we will be better prepared to love others.

8. Love is Not Easily Angered

Anger is a strong emotion of displeasure, hostility or annoyance. It is often provoked internally. However, external factors can also stimulate this feeling. There is nothing wrong with any emotion. Anger is one of God's created emotions. It can be constructive and destructive depending on the motive. Anger is constructive when used to cause positive changes such as fighting injustice, racism, discrimination and protecting human rights.

It can also be deadly when it is not managed effectively, such as hurting someone or for vengeful purposes. Even in healthy relationships, anger can be expressed, although it should not be a common occurrence. If so, it must be addressed immediately.

There may be underlying issues for frequent angry outbursts. Anger must be managed effectively. For example, if I physically hurt someone because I am feeling angry, my anger is not being used constructively. It can even be a criminal offense. I can be charged with assault and battery. Obviously, this is not an acceptable way of managing my anger. Instead of acting on my anger in this manner, I can wait until I am able to be civil and express my emotion effectively.

God's love is not easily annoyed, but it is patient. Likewise, if we want to develop healthy relationships, we must learn to manage our anger effectively. These scriptures shed some light on how to deal with anger:

"Be angry, and do not sin: do not let the sun go down on your wrath, nor give place to the devil. Let him who stole steal no longer, but rather let him labor, working with his hands what is good, that he may have something to give him who has need. Let no corrupt word proceed out of your mouth, but what is good for necessary edification, that it may impart grace to the hearers. And do not grieve the Holy Spirit of God, by whom you were sealed for the day of redemption. Let all bitterness, wrath, anger, clamor, and evil speaking be put away from you, with all malice" (*Ephesians 4:26-31*).

9. Love Keeps No Records

Love does not keep an accounting record of all wrongs. Instead, love forgives all. Those who practice love choose to forgive their friends' offenses, and undergo a healing process to restore their relationships.

10. Love Does Not Delight in Evil, but Rejoices with the Truth

Those who practice love do not rejoice in evil. They are hurt when their family, friends and others are in pain. They cry with their friends when they are crying, and rejoice when they are rejoicing. Love feels joyful with honesty, sincerity and truth.

11. Love Always Protects

God's love covers all sins. God's love is patient, and it holds back His wrath. He protects his children from harm. King David said, "If it had not been the Lord who was on our side, when men rose up against us, then they would have swallowed us alive when their wrath was kindled against us; Then the waters would have overwhelmed us, the stream would have gone over our soul; Then the swollen waters would have gone over our soul" *(Psalms 124:2-5).*

> **Love feels joyful with honesty, sincerity and truth.**

Likewise, we must learn to protect our family, friends and others. This includes protecting them from spiritual, psychological, physical, financial and other vulnerabilities. Parents must protect their children; husbands and wives must protect their spouses; and everyone must protect their friends and neighbors, for tomorrow they may be the ones protecting you.

12. Love Always Trusts
Trust is a firm reliance on the integrity, ability or character of a person or thing. In healthy relationships, trust is a vital key, because no relationship can grow without it. There is a process to trusting a new friend, for trust is earned over time. The closer you get to your friends or loved ones, the easier it will be to trust them

13. Love Always Hopes
Hope is the desire to achieve a goal, or to expect something to happen. Hope empowers us to take action to achieve a definite goal. "Hope deferred makes the heart sick, but when the desire comes, it is a tree of life" (*Proverbs 13:12*). Therefore, love always hopes for the best to happen. God hopes for the best for His children. He wants all His children to be saved. It is recorded, "Even so it is not the will of your Father who is in heaven that one of these little ones should perish" (*Matthew 18:14*).

In your relationships, I encourage you to have hope and speak hopeful words to inspire your loved ones.

14. Love Always Perseveres

Perseverance is the continued effort to think and act toward the attainment of an aim despite difficulties, discouragement and temporary setbacks. If you are seeking your soul mate or other healthy relationships, I encourage you to be patient and pursue your desires persistently. If you do, they will be achieved. If you continue to delight yourself in the Lord, He will give you the desires of your heart. God's love will empower you to pursue your dreams despite hardships.

15. Love Never Fails

God's love never fails and never disappoints. "Behold, he who keeps Israel shall neither slumber nor sleep" (*Psalms 121:4*). We may disobey Him, but He never stops loving us. He is always ready to give us a helping hand when we fall. Even when we walk away from Him, He is receptive to welcome those who repent and are ready to return home. The parable of The Lost Son is a great example of God's love. You can read the story in the book of *Luke, 15:11-32*.

Love will never disappoint or prove undependable on a consistent basis. God's love prevails to eternity. Apostle Paul wrote: "For I am persuaded that neither death nor life, nor angels, nor principalities, nor powers, nor things present, nor things to come, nor height nor depth, nor any other created thing shall be able to separate us from the love of God, which is in Christ Jesus our Lord" (*Romans 8:38-39*). If we want to develop healthy relationships, we must learn to practice love. It is the pillar for all relationships. If we meditate on these lessons we will be nourished and empowered to love ourselves, God and others forever.

Love is a human need. Your loved ones *expect* your love. If you want to establish and maintain healthy relationships, treat people as you would want them to treat you. Love is so important that God made it into a commandment. "You shall love the Lord your God with all your heart, with all your soul, and with your entire mind. This is the first and greatest commandment. And the second is like it: 'You shall love your neighbor as yourself" (*Matthew 22:37-39*). I encourage you to continuously learn to love yourself, God and others. When you love others, you will also increase in love. For that which you sow, you will also reap.

It is important to note that while it is God's commandment to love and help our loved ones, we must not let anyone take advantage of our love. The help you give to a friend must be done in the context of love and wisdom. For example, if one of my friends is sick, I will visit, I'll call, I'll pray and I'll help financially when possible. However, I am not expected to exhaust all of my resources to help everyone. I also do not expect my loved ones to be responsible for my life. We all have our own responsibilities and loads to carry. We are not required to help beyond our resources. Your friends' urgency or lack of planning should not be *your* emergency. In healthy friendships each party has their choices and consequences. Each member understands their personal boundaries and responsibilities.

If you or your friends lack boundaries, I recommend the book "Boundaries" by Dr. Henry Cloud. This book helped me to set proper boundaries in my relationships. For example, I use to give free advice to friends who were not available for me when I needed them most. After reading Dr. Cloud's book and applying its key principles I am now comfortable saying "No" to friends and others when it is appropriate. My life was chaotic prior to grasping the concept of boundaries. I placed my own needs and desires on hold for others. However, the return on that investment was very low. Dr. Cloud's book helped me to take control of my life by teaching me how to set proper boundaries with people. My life is getting to a manageable state. I am now better equipped to pursue my writing career and other goals.

My prayer is that you will continue to love others as yourself. The more you love and accept yourself, the easier it will be to love others. When you love people, you allow them to be who they are. People like to be comfortable and free to think, feel and act as they please. If you want healthy relationships, you must let your friends and loved ones express themselves freely. They will never be perfect. However, you can choose to accept your friends as they are. Since they accept you as *you* are, extend the same grace.

Remember, you can only give who you are in a meaningful relationship. You can only love to the extent that you love yourself. You can only help your loved ones when you are well. I want to leave this chapter with a quote by Carl R. Rogers: *"People are just as wonderful as sunsets if you let them be. When I look at a sunset, I don't find myself saying, 'Soften the orange a bit on the right hand corner.' I don't try to control a sunset. I watch with awe as it unfolds."*

Step 5 Summary

Love is not just a feeling, but it is sacrificial. Love is best expressed in giving and doing for yourself, God and others. "Love is patient, love is kind. It does not envy, it does not boast, it is not proud. It does not dishonor others, it is not self-seeking, it is not easily angered, and it keeps no record of wrongs. Love does not delight in evil but rejoices with the truth. It always protects, always trusts, always hopes and always perseveres. Love never fails..." (*1 Corinthians 13:4-8*).

God *is* love, and He wants to lavish His love on *you*. If the Holy Spirit of God lives in you, you'll walk in love. Your actions will be based on love and wisdom. If you are looking for love, consider going to the source. Ask God to fill you with his love. He will freely give you the love your heart desires.

I conclude this step with the following take-aways:

1. Love is earned over time.
2. Love is mutually beneficial.
3. Love is a choice, not just a feeling.
4. Love yourself, love God and love others, for love is the pillar of all healthy relationships.
5. Love can be increased through the process of self-discovery, acceptance and practice.

The time is **NOW** for you to love others as they want to be loved. Also, ask them to love you as you want to be loved! Love is a choice and not just a feeling!

Step 6

Become Trustworthy

> *"Trust men and they will be true to you; treat them greatly and they will show themselves great."*
>
> Emerson

D o you find it difficult to trust? If so, you are not alone. There are many people who face this challenge every day. Sometimes we do not even know why it is difficult to trust. We were all created with the basic ability to trust. We were born to trust ourselves and others. However, the experiences in life and our reaction to them provide the fertile ground for mistrust. In this step we'll examine the following tenets of trust:

- The meaning of trust
- 3 Benefits of trust
- 3 causes of mistrust
- 5 Tips to build trust in your relationships

The Meaning of Trust

Trust is essential for building healthy relationships. Without this foundation, no relationship can really endure. Trust is to a relationship as oxygen is to the body. All healthy relationships must be based on mutual trust in order to grow and thrive. Trust is both an emotional and a rational act. Emotionally, it is where we openly expose our vulnerabilities to people, and believe they will not take advantage of our honesty. Rationally, it is where we have calculated the probabilities of gain and loss based on previous experiences and data that leads to the conclusion that the person in question will behave appropriately.

Trust is love. Trust is a firm reliance on the integrity, ability or character of a person or thing. It is having confidence in something or someone. It is self-confidence. It is the ability to depend on someone despite knowing the possibility of failure. It is the ability to depend on God by faith. However, to trust others you must first learn to trust yourself. The big question is: Why is it important to trust yourself and others?

In building healthy relationships, self-trust must be established before you can effectively trust others. The truth is that nobody can truly trust others without the ability to first trust themselves. We can only offer what we have and who we are. If we cannot trust ourselves, we cannot trust others, and if we cannot trust others, we will not be able to trust God. Again, trust is love. If we want to develop healthy relationships, we must learn to love by practicing trust.

I believe that self-trust is the process of knowing ourselves and accepting who God created us to be. Self-trust is faith. It is the reliance on one's integrity, strength and ability. It is a mental stage or condition of being confident. In the words of Emerson: *"Self-trust is the first secret of success."* When we trust ourselves, we will find it easier to trust God and others. If we allow God, He will empower us to trust. If we do not have self-trust, we cannot extend it to others, for we can only give that which we have. If we desire healthy relationships, we must first learn to trust ourselves and others. In *my* experience of self-discovery, I learned that the more self-aware I become, the easier it is to trust.

The process to self-trust consists of knowing and accepting who we are. Trust is learned over time. We must possess it before we can trust others. This is why I recommend seeking self-awareness, and learn to trust yourself before pursuing healthy relationships.

While you are learning to trust yourself and others, it is important to remember that it takes time. Thus, I urge you to be patient and gracious. The process of learning to trust is different for each person. For example, my process took longer, since I have many interpersonal conflicts to deal with, and was not taught how to trust as a child. However, it may be easier and quicker for you to trust if you *were* taught how to trust as a child, and adopt a positive mindset that fosters trusting relationships.

This initial step toward self-trust is to know ourselves. The second step is to accept ourselves. While we can change many aspects of our lives, there are certain aspects that cannot be changed. Thus, we need the empowerment of God to change what we can, the wisdom to accept what we cannot, and surrender them to God. In my process of self-acceptance, I often pray Reinhold Niebuhr's Serenity Prayer, and believe that you may find it helpful as well: "*God, grant me the serenity to accept the things I cannot change, the courage to change the things I can, and the wisdom to know the difference.*"

As I learn to trust myself, I also learn from God and others. I learn how to take care of myself with confidence and independence. To manage my life effectively I am learning to develop **S**pecific, **M**easureable, **A**chievable, **R**eachable and **T**imely (**SMART**) plans to maximize my strengths. My desire is to do what I can do to achieve my life purpose, and let God do His part in my life. I am also learning to better manage my weaknesses by seeking help from friends and family members. (My wife also keeps me out of trouble. I am blessed to have a wonderful friend and life partner!) My prayer is that everyone will find at least three meaningful friends they can trust and share the joys and the pains of life with. The journey of life is not intended to be taken alone, and we all benefit from healthy relationships.

3 Benefits of Trust

What benefits are you enjoying for trusting your loved ones? Making a list will give you a new perspective on the benefits of your relationships. There are many benefits to be gained by trusting people.

1. Trust helps us develop bonds with each other. Bonding is the connection of identity between two or more people where each person connects their *self* to that of the other person or group. People who are bonded care about one another and naturally trust one another.

2. Trust helps us build healthy relationships with anyone we desire. To build healthy relationships we need to trust. Trust is built on healthy relationships. If you want to develop healthy relationships, you must learn to trust yourself and others. As you learn to trust others, I advise that you do so in the context of love and wisdom.

This means that you do not have to trust *everyone*. You must choose those you feel are trustworthy. A great place to start practicing trust is with those who love you. How do you know who loves you? You must verify what they say and do. They must their worth to be in your circle of healthy friendships.

> *"A blessed thing it is for any man or woman to have a friend, one human soul whom we can trust utterly, who knows the best and worst of us, and who loves us in spite of all our faults."*
>
> Charles Kingsley

Trust affects your relationships at home and at work. When your clients trust you, they will buy from you. As you continue to build trust at your workplace and properly promote your services and products, your sales will increase. People do business with those they like and trust.

We all need mutual cooperation to create greater success. Nobody can succeed alone. We need others to build a mastermind and help us achieve our goals. Even Jesus Christ used a team to achieve His purpose on earth. As God, He could do anything He wanted. Yet, He chose to partner and shared His ministry with His disciples. He had the twelve disciples to help Him with His passion to save the world. He said, "I have come that they may have life, and that they may have it more abundantly" (*John 10:10*). He partnered with the initial twelve disciples and others to reach out to the world. Therefore, if we want to succeed in play, in business and in life, we must learn to trust certain people and develop alliances with them to achieve enduring success.

3. Trust affects your relationship with God. The Bible emphasizes the importance of trusting our creator. However, we must all decide whether to trust God by faith. Since the Creator is an invisible being, we can only trust through the process of faith. What is faith? "Now faith is the substance of things hoped for, the evidence of things not seen" (*Hebrews 11:1*). Why trust God? The answer is really simple because He *is* trustworthy. You can trust that God will do what He says. "God is not a man, that He should lie, nor a son of man, that He should repent. Has He said, and will He not do? Or has He spoken, and will He not make it good?" (*Numbers 23:19-19*).

Trust is earned through the process of verifying what is said and the actions that follow. The wisdom of Ronald Reagan taught us to "trust, but verify" everything. This principle even applies to our Creator. In fact, everything He commands always comes to pass. He said that He loves humanity and gave His only son to die for the sins of the world. He promised to bless Abraham, who then became a blessed man. The same will be true for you. If God says He will bless you, you can trust His Word. The Word of God is bound. The Bible contains many examples of God's trustworthiness. He always comes through. He is never too late. He is not limited by our time. He never fails, for He is love. He is always there even if you do not feel Him. The fact that the sun rises every morning is a sign that you can trust God to keep His Word.

In life you may fall and others may fail, but God never fails.

Trust is so important that our God commands us to trust Him. Healthy relationships cannot be developed without trust in God. "Trust in the Lord with all your heart, and lean not on your own understanding; in all your ways acknowledge Him, and He shall direct your paths" (*Proverbs 3:5-6*).

There is nothing wrong with trusting yourself and others, but it is far more important to trust God, because He is infallible. In life you may fall and others may fail, but God never fails. He may choose not to answer you when and how you want, but His love never fails His children. He will never abandon you. "Be strong and of good courage, do not fear nor be afraid of them; for the Lord your God, He is the One who goes with you. He will not leave you nor forsake you" (*Deuteronomy 31:6*).

If you feel that God has forgotten you, you can "remind" Him in prayer and by meditating on His word. I recommend meditating on these Biblical references: *Psalms 37:28, Psalms 27:10, Joshua 1:5* and *Hebrews 13:5*. Prayer is a process to remind *us* of things through our conversations with God. If you desire to learn more about prayer and praying effectively, please read my book "Prayer: How to Develop a Personal Relationship with God."

Now that you understand the meaning of trust, let us explore some of the reasons it is difficult to trust.

| **All things are possible for those who believe and take action to achieve their goals.** |

What are *your* reasons for not trusting some people? I believe there are many. In this section we will focus on three common causes of mistrust:

- Childhood trauma
- Mindset
- Fear

1. Childhood Trauma

In my graduate studies I read and studied various theories on childhood development. They included works by psychologists such as Freud, Erikson, Piaget and Kohlberg. They all agreed that early childhood development impacts people's ability to trust and build healthy relationships. I like Erikson's theory because it covers our lifespan development. It is comprehensive and offers the framework to continue to grow even if we failed to master certain stages along the way. Erikson's Stages of Development will be presented later in this section.

Nevertheless, no matter how challenging your early childhood may have been, I want to encourage that it is never too late for a new beginning. There is always hope to improve. Your life can be transformed over time. As you change your mindset and pursue your goals, your life will be changed!

You do not need a degree in clinical social work, psychology or any of the related social sciences to understand that traumas—particularly childhood traumas—can adversely affect a person's ability to trust. Generally, children are vulnerable, lack wisdom and have not developed the necessary coping skills to manage traumatic life events. For example, a girl who was sexually abused by her father may have a harder time trusting men if the psychological effects of the trauma are not addressed.

Trust and social interactions are crucial in healthy human development. Social interactions can greatly influence a person's core values, beliefs, emotions and even their ability to trust. If basic trust is not mastered, mistrust will be established as a result. If you have experienced life events that created mistrust, there is hope for you. With new information and association with loving people you can learn to trust again. Remember, all things are possible for those who believe and take action to achieve their goals.

While early childhood traumas can negatively impact one's trusting capability for several years, it does not have to be a permanent condition. I believe that there is always hope for a positive change. People continue to grow and develop throughout their lives. If your past is holding you back from your destiny, I encourage you to seek healing from God, and seek support from loving people.

In addition, a professional counselor or pastor may be helpful for some people. If you seek professional counseling, please be sure that you are ready and willing to change. It will save you time and money. Professional counseling is more effective when the individual seeking help is ready and willing to pursue it diligently. I highly recommend prayer as a means to draw closer to God. Ask Him for help with any painful experiences. He declared: "Ask and it will be given to you; seek, and you will find; knock and it will be opened to you" (*Matthew 7:7*).

The main principle of "ask, seek and knock" is to do so earnestly until you find the answers you seek.

Do not allow past experiences to stop you from trusting and enjoying life.

I like the saying, *"A quitter never wins, and a winner never quits."* Meditation is also helpful to reduce stress and to reach out to the supernatural world. I urge you to not allow past experiences to stop you from trusting and enjoying life. Do not dwell in the past. The present is momentary; it is all you have now, therefore, make the best of it. The future is a mystery; there is no need to worry about it. You simply need to plan and pray for the best. As the saying goes: *"If you fail to plan, you plan to fail."*

2. Mindset

What is mindset? It's a mental operating system. It is our belief system, our worldview and the way we see ourselves and others. Our mindsets are our thinking centers that determine our behaviors, results and who we are. "For as he thinks in his heart, so is he..." (*Proverbs 23:7*).

Our mindsets are influenced by both nature and nurture. For example, our nature determines our biological makeup such as DNA programming, gender, skin color and height. The aspects of the environment influences on our mindsets include where we live, schools we attend and the friends we have. Dr. Lauretta Justin said, *"When we combine our nature and nurture, we get certain voices; and these voices create our mindsets or belief system."* On a recent presentation I attended, Dr. Justin outlined three voices that influence our mindsets: authority, peer influence and perception. The mindsets we hold determine our ability to trust. Therefore, it is important to examine the voices that influence *your* "trust muscle" to ensure that they are based on truth, and not on outdated, irrelevant and faulty information.

Fixed Mindset vs. Growth Mindset

In the book "Mindset: The New Psychology of Success," Dr. Carol Dweck described two types of mindset: the fixed mindset, and the growth mindset. This discovery was a result of decades of social science research. This book is a must-read for all who want to develop healthy relationships and succeed in life.

Fixed Mindset
People who adopt a fixed mindset think differently than those with a growth mindset. Here are some of the beliefs of the people with a fixed mindset:

- They believe that their intelligence is fixed, with little hope for growth. This belief leads to the desire to *look* smart rather than *being* smart. People who hold this mindset avoid challenges necessary for growth.
- They subconsciously give up easily when life's obstacles knock at their door.
- They believe that efforts are useless.
- They do not welcome criticism.
- They often get jealous or envy the success of others.
- They live a life of fear and regret.
- They view setbacks and limitations as permanent conditions instead of temporary defeats. This limited thinking makes it difficult to ever achieve greater success, joy and happiness.

Growth Mindset

The following qualities represent those who hold the growth mindset:

- They believe that their basic traits and intelligence are dynamic. It can be developed over time with the right training and persistence. This belief leads to the desire to learn and grow. People who hold this type of mindset embrace challenges necessary for growth.
- They are positive thinkers.
- They take actions toward achieving their purpose and goals.
- They are willing to learn and grow every day.
- They are more likely to see the cup half full rather than   half empty.
- They are most likely to see and create opportunities out of life challenges rather than complaining of lack of opportunities.
- They often have high standards for living.
- They have faith and hope for a better tomorrow.
- They often have a strategy or a written plan to succeed instead of living by chance.
- They don't avert challenges, but face their problems squarely, seeking solutions to overcome them. They are likely to learn lesson from their problems and turn their setbacks into comebacks.

If you have adopted the fixed mindset I encourage you to shift your focus to the growth mindset. You will find better results in life. Everyday life will be much more pleasant and enjoyable.

I believe that if you change your mindset and take positive actions toward your goals, you will change your life and improve your relationships. You can change any mindset if you want to. However, the need to change must be a recognized priority. God has given you the power to change your life. If you believe it and take action toward your goal, you *will* change your life.

The mindset change cycle below illustrates the flow of changing your mindset, and requires a step by step commitment.

The Mindset Change Cycle

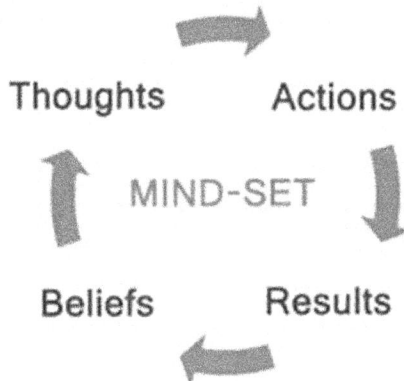

Thoughts   Actions

MIND-SET

Beliefs   Results

It's always a process to change from a negative mindset to a positive mindset. It takes willingness and effort. Your desire to change must also be greater than your desire to stay the same.

The process of changing your mindset begins by deciding and controlling what goes into your mind. This is important because what you regularly hear, focus and meditate on w will impact your belief. You are consistently exposed to millions of negative messages. Quite often these massages can be overpowering, which is why you must choose what enters your mind. You have the power to choose what enters your mind.

> *"To change your life, you have to change yourself. To change yourself, you have to change your mindset."*
> Wilson Kanadi

5 Tips to Change Your Mindset and Your Life

1. Acknowledgement
Acknowledge your limiting mindset. Take inventory of your thinking and feelings to ensure they are consistent with your current goals.

2. Decision
Make the decision that you *want* to change your limited thinking.

3. New perspective
Get a new perspective by getting new information to replace the old thinking. Having a life coach or a mentor is very helpful. They can help to reframe your unwanted thinking.

4. Self-Care
One of the best ways to change your thinking is to change   your physiology. When you take great care of your body, it positively affects your entire life.

5. Plan for Success
Success in any area of life requires planning. If you want healthier relationships, you must plan for it. You can start getting a relationship coach.

As your coach, I'll help you define your vision, set smart goals and develop a plan to achieve EXTRAORDINARY results. To learn more about our coaching program, visit CoachJamesJustin.com!

Bonus Tip

Here's a quick exercise that can help when you're feeling nervous about trying something new: Rub your hands as fast as you can and clap them as hard as you can. Repeat this at least three times and you will instantly feel better!

Here's another tip: You must commit to and develop the environment that fosters high standards for continued education, growth and development. As you continue to change your mindset and take action toward achieving your goals, your life will be transformed! If you feel that you need additional support, tools and help to achieve your goals, email me by visiting CoachJamesJustin.com.

3. Fear

Fear is the third most common cause of mistrust in relationships. It impedes our ability to develop healthy relationships. If you allow your fears to control you, they will rob your joy every day. Fear is an emotion that alerts us to threats and dangers. There are two types of fear: the rational, and the irrational.

The rational fear is the responsible emotion that empowers us to be cautious and respectable, and show reverence to authorities. This includes the fear we have for our parents, God and other authorities. This type of fear is based on love and wisdom.

In contrast, irrational fear has no basis for it torments.

Irrational fear paralyzes us from pursuing our dreams.

It paralyzes us from pursuing our dreams. It is true that everyone will experience fearful events in life. These events invite fear. They impact our ability to trust other, ourselves and even God. However, we do not have to let our fears stop us from enjoying life. I believe that we have the power to overcome our fears. No matter what happened in our past, we can overcome them with God's help and with help from loving people. This is another great reason to develop healthy relationships. Together we will overcome our fears and pursue our dreams! The spirit of fear is a liar, and we will not listen to its lies anymore. In love we are free from fear, for perfect love drives out fears.

Remember, the **F.E.A.R** acronym stands for **F**alse **E**vidence **A**ppearing **R**eal. The irrational fears are usually based on a faulty **B**elief **S**ystem or fixed mindset that we developed from wrong information and teaching.

When we focus on fear with the lens of love and truth, it seems to weaken and disappear. Do not believe the voice of fear that tells you it is impossible and that you cannot trust anyone. It is a lie. Again, nothing is impossible to those who believe. If you believe, you will achieve your heart's desires. Your dreams *can* come true as you continue to believe and not bow to fear.

| If you believe, you will achieve! |

If fear has knocked you down, you can get back up again. If you need a helping hand, it is okay to ask for it. There are more than enough people who are willing to love you and build healthy relationships with you. Therefore, please do not let fear stop you. Even if you cannot see a way out of your misery, and some people have violated your trust, I encourage you to get up and move forward. You can learn to trust your dreams again and trust others to help you achieve your dreams.

7 Tips to Build Trust in Your Relationships

Trust is essential to build healthy relationships. The more you learn to trust yourself, the easier it will be to trust others. If you cannot trust yourself, you cannot trust others. If you cannot trust others, then your relationships will be shallow. Building trust takes time, especially when one or both parties have been hurt in the past. Here are seven practical tips to develop trust in relationships:

1. **Become trustworthy in the little things.**
   If people can trust you with little things, they will eventually trust you with their lives. The best group of people with whom to practice trust is your family. You can start by keeping small promises such as returning a call when agreed to do so. The Bible declares, *"Whoever can be trusted with very little can also be trusted with much, and whoever is dishonest with very little will also be dishonest with much. So if you have not been trustworthy in handling worldly wealth, who will trust you with true riches?" (Luke 16:10-11).*

   Again, healthy relationships are based on mutual trust. People need to be able to trust you in the little things before they can trust you with the big things. For example, if you promised to take a friend out, be sure to keep the promise. If a person cannot trust you to show up on time or remember to do something that you promised to do, why should they trust you with something more meaningful?

2. **Spend time with the other person.**
It takes time to build trust. If you want to build trust in any relationship you must spend time with the one you desire to have a relationship with. In this era of text messaging and email it can be easy to spend very little "real" time with the people you love.

3. **Share personal information about yourself.**
If you want to develop healthy relationships, you will have to work at it over time. It is important to spend time with those you want to build a relationship and share your heart with. Believe it or not, they cannot read your mind; you must tell them what is in your heart and allow them to share with you. Healthy relationships need to be reciprocal. If you want to build trust in a relationship you need to become vulnerable yourself. You should not ask your friends for what you are not willing to give.

4. **Confidentiality.**
This is a big deal in any relationship. In counseling, it is an ethical code that must not be violated except in the case of a court order, or in the event the client is at risk to themselves or others. In friendly relationships, keep the other

person's confidence by not sharing confidential conversations with anyone else. What a person tells you in secret must stay in that relationship. Likewise, your information must be kept confidential as well. If someone cannot keep your information confidentially, it may be time to find someone else.

5. **Do not be selfish; consider the needs of others.**
Do things that are in the best interest of other people. Remember, mistrust is often learned in dysfunctional relationships. Trust, however, can only be learned in *healthy* relationships. If you want to build trust in a relationship, you need to make choices that are beneficial to yourself *and* the best interest of others. If you consider the needs of others, they are more likely to consider *your* needs in return.

6. **Apologize when you are wrong.**
As mortals we all make mistakes. However, we cannot use nature as an excuse to *continue* making mistakes. We must learn to apologize, admit when we are wrong and ask for forgiveness. If you want to build self-trust and trust in others, you must learn to *forgive* yourself and others. Nothing shatters trust faster than hurting others and refusing to apologize and change. I urge you to forgive others even when they are wrong. Forgiveness is not about others; it is about your freedom.

7. **Laughter.**
   Please feel free to laugh at your silliness! Life is too short not to laugh at funny things. Laughter is great medicine for the soul. If you can learn to laugh at yourself and others' silliness, you can learn to trust.

Step 6 Summary

What does trust mean to you? Trust is both an emotional and a rational act. Emotionally it is where we expose our vulnerabilities openly to people and believe they will not take advantage of our honesty. Rationally it is where we have calculated the probabilities of gain and loss based on previous experiences and data that leads to the conclusion that the person in question will behave appropriately. Trust is love. Trust is a firm reliance on the integrity, ability or character of a person or thing. It is having confidence in something or someone. It is self-confidence. It is the ability to depend on someone despite knowing the possibility of failure.

| **Trust is a vital key in all relationships.** |

Trust is a vital key in all healthy relationships. Trust is to healthy relationships as oxygen is to the body. Without this key, no relationship can grow. Trust is earned over time. It is okay to trust others, but you must inspect all things. The more you trust yourself, the easier it will get to trust others. As you get closer to your loved ones, it will be easier to trust them.

If you are having difficulty trusting some people, it is best to check yourself and trust your instincts. Fear is perhaps the leading cause of mistrust. Fear is best addressed in a healthy relationship. There is no fear in love, for it eliminates fear and doubts.

There are many ways to strengthen your trust muscle. However, the best and quickest way is to develop healthy relationships. Mistrust is often learned in dysfunctional relationships, but it can be un-learned by changing the negative mindset, and by being in healthy relationships.

I appreciate President Reagan's philosophy to "trust, but verify" everything. People often do what is *inspected* rather than what is *expected*. That is why I recommend that you trust your team, but verify what they do.

Step 7

Become Committed

> *"Desire is the key to motivation, but it's determination and commitment to an unrelenting pursuit of your goal—a commitment to excellence—that will enable you to attain the success you seek."*
>
> Mario Andretti

How committed are you in your relationships? On a scale of 1-10, where 1 represents no commitment, and 10 means that you are 100 percent committed to those you are in relationships with, where are you? Hold on to your answer until you read this step. It will give you a clearer understanding of commitment, why sometime it is difficult to commit and how you can improve your commitment level in your relationships.

> **Show me your commitment by what you say, and I will show you my commitment by what I do.**

In relationship building, commitment description varies from person to person. While our definition may be different, commitment remains an essential key for developing all healthy relationships. Indeed, it's the solid foundation for establishing and maintaining *healthy* relationships. In my opinion, nobody can build healthy relationships without it.

Commitment is an act of love whereby an individual willingly agrees to perform a task (Merriam-Webster). Commitment in any relationship is best demonstrated by actions. This is why I often say to my friends, show me your commitment by what you say, and I will show you my commitment by what I do. Essentially, commitment without works is dead. Commitment is action-based rather than mere words. The level of commitment required to build healthy relationships is similar to the commitment of a parent to a child, a husband to a wife and God to His children. This level of commitment is based on love, trust, loyalty, wisdom and reciprocity. Let's review 3 major reasons why commitment is a challenge for some people.

3 Reasons Why Commitment is Vital

There are many reasons why it is difficult for some people to commit. From my coaching business I have observed the following three factors:

1. Fear

From my studies and experience as a counselor, I discovered that fear is a primary reason some people shy away from commitment. They are afraid of being hurt. They often think that opening their hearts to a relationship (again) may be too risky. Therefore, in order to protect themselves they keep their hearts closed.

Fear to commit often exists as a result of past hurts. The human rationale encourages self-protection through emotional isolation, and by using certain emotional defenses. While it may be helpful to use emotional defenses to cope with fear, it should not be a permanent solution.

If you were hurt in a relationship, it is best to address it before pursuing healthy relationship. Your fear of being hurt again will impede your effort to build healthy relationships. How do you get help? My recommendation is to hire a professional counselor or a coach. I also recommend that you surround yourself with loving people for natural help.

One of the best solutions to overcome fear is God's love. Engaging in relationship with people is a great way to practice love. Love is very important in dealing with fear. It empowers us to face our fears. *"There is no fear in love; but perfect love casts out fear..." (1 John 4:18, NKJV).*

Anyone who shies away from commitment due to unresolved fear will not be able to develop healthy relationships. Anyone who wants to develop healthy relationships must overcome their fear and take calculated risks to build new relationships.

> *"I learned that courage was not the absence of fear, but the triumph over it. The brave man is not he who does not feel afraid, but he who conquers that fear."*
>
> Nelson Mandela

A successful or enlightened life is all about taking calculated risks. The people who take more risks often achieve more. They learn to act even when they are afraid. They accept that each life experience is an opportunity for learning.

The same is true in relationships. The current relationships you have can be opportunities for future relationships. If you want to overcome fear of commitment, you must develop courage, take calculated risks and start new relationships. I encourage you to start with small commitments and work your way up to bigger ones. Remember, commitment is best expressed in healthy relationships.

2. Low self-esteem

Low self-esteem is a depressed perception of a person's overall emotional evaluation of their own worth. It is a result of various factors including physical appearance or weight, socioeconomic status, peer pressure or bullying. A person with low self-esteem may exhibit some of the following characteristics:

- Heavy self-criticism and dissatisfaction
- Perception that temporary setbacks are permanent, intolerable conditions
- Hypersensitivity to criticism, with resentment against critics and feelings of being attacked
- Chronic indecision, and an exaggerated fear of mistakes
- Excessive will to please and seeking approval from others
- Perfectionism, which can lead to frustration when perfection is not achieved
- Envy or general resentment

People who suffer from low self-esteem do not believe that they are good enough to be in a meaningful or healthy relationship. They do not feel they have anything to offer in a relationship. They are often full of self-contempt, and though they may have much strength, they do not see it in themselves. The strengths they have are covered under their negative self-talk. If this is your case, there is good news: You have the power to change your life by changing your mindset to a positive one!

You can start by completing a self-esteem assessment, and developing a plan to increase your self-esteem. If you feel it will help, you can seek guidance from a professional counselor and surround yourself with loving people. If you spend much of your time in an environment where you do not have many positive people around, you can start reading the Bible and other books that build up your spirit, soul and body. It is also helpful to be patient, for it takes time to build higher self-esteem.

3. Lack of experience
Commitment is like a muscle: The more it is used, the stronger it gets. If you are new at making commitments, I recommend that you start small and make bigger commitments as your confidence increases. Begin the process by making and keeping promises to your family, friends and co-workers. Your loved ones and co-workers are great people to exercise your commitment muscle. They are more likely to forgive you quicker and coach you objectively.

> **When you know your strengths and limitations, you will commit according to your resources.**

If it is true that practice makes perfect, then we can all agree that we will get better as we increase our commitments. I encourage you to experiment with making different commitments, and do your best to keep them. If you are unable to keep a promise, you owe it to yourself to apologize and ask for forgiveness. If you are unable to keep a scheduled appointment with your loved ones, it is best to call in advance to cancel. This demonstrates that you are respectable and responsible. As you learn to commit, I encourage you to be patient and ask for help when you need it.

How to Improve Commitment in Your Relationships

It is helpful to commit to the right cause or to the right person, and more fun to keep a promise to someone or something you believe in and love. The level of enthusiasm will be higher if you believe in what you have promised. The load is also lighter when it is shared evenly. It is helpful to commit to something or someone with a higher return on investment. For example, it is a joy to keep my promises to my spouse, for we have a healthy relationship. We both invest seriously in each other. We use the following components in our continued quest to maintain and enrich our commitment to each other:

- **Patience**
  In a healthy relationship it takes time to make the right commitments. Do not rush into a

commitment if you are not ready. Take your time and keep your promises. It is best to make no commitments to anyone unless you have the means and intent to keep your promises.

- **Trust in Yourself**
  Trust yourself. In relationships, you must trust yourself. If you are wrong sometimes, it is okay. But if you trust yourself you will be happier. It is best to let your "yes" be yes and your "no" be no. People will respect you more when you have the courage to keep your word. Trust yourself and trust that God will lead you to the truth. You have to learn to take a risk in relationships. You will never have all the facts to commit. You have to learn to trust that things will go the way they are desired and according to your plan. You may not—and should not—be able to control everything. However, you *do* have control over your commitment level in a relationship, and the types of company you keep.

- **Becoming Self-Aware**
  It is easier to commit when you know who you are. When you know your strengths and limitations you will commit according to your resources. You will be better prepared to maximize your strengths and seek help for your weaknesses, and better able to express yourself openly with those in your life.

- **Making Use of Previous Relationships**
  When you are trying to increase your commitment level it is helpful to take inventory of your past relationships. Whether they were good or bad experiences, they were opportunities to learn. What have you learned about commitment from previous relationships, and how are you using these lessons to improve your current relationships? Take a closer look at your past relationships with people you really loved, and replicate the useful lessons in current relationships.

- **Getting Help**
  We all need help sometimes. If you are struggling with commitment or any difficulty in life, please get help from your loved ones and professionals. It is hurtful to yourself if you do not seek help when you need it.

Step 7 Summary

You have the power to create what our heart desires. However, you must plan, prepare and commit to a definite goal. If you want to establish and maintain healthy relationship, you must commit to it.

> **Commitment is not a chore. It is a *choice* supported by action.**

Commitment is a mental state, dedication and the act of pursuing and achieving a desire. Much like a muscle, the more you practice it, the stronger you'll become. Commitment is the required fuel to healthy relationships. Whatsoever we desire, we must be willing to work for. There is nothing free in life. Commitment is not a chore. It is a choice supported by action. It is based on love, wisdom, respect and reciprocity. If you want others to commit to *you*, you must first commit to *them*.

In the beginning of this step, I asked you rate your commitment level in your relationships. Take time now to reflect on your commitment skills. I encourage you to define what commitment means to you, why it is sometimes difficult to commit, and practice the tips you have learned to improve these skills. The more you practice the skills of commitment, the easier it will be. Remember, you have the power to create what you want. If you want healthy relationships, you must commit in your pursuit!

Conclusion

We know that developing, nurturing and maintaining healthy relationships is important in life. Healthy relationships are an enriching and vital component of our success, happiness and quality of life, both personally and professionally. Embracing our friendships help us to achieve our goals, supports us in times of need and allows us to experience a dynamic source of love and support.

**Everything you want is within your reach!
If you have the right mindset and take the right action, you WILL achieve your goals.**

Relationship is a basic human need. We all want to belong, loved and accepted. We want to be *celebrated*, not just *tolerated*. As Franklin D. Roosevelt so aptly phrased: *"If civilization is to survive, we must cultivate the science of human relationships—the ability of all peoples, of all kinds, to live together, in the same world at peace."*

In this book you were introduced to the Justin's 7 Steps to Develop Healthy Relationships with Anyone. These steps are as follows:

1. Become Self-Aware
2. Become Selective
3. Become the Friend You Want to Attract

4. Become an Effective Communicator
5. Become Loving
6. Become Trustworthy
7. Become Committed

These steps are designed to equip you with the most effective tools to achieve your relationship goals. These steps will transform your relationships and your life!

They helped me improve my marriage and other relationships. My clients are utilizing these 7 steps toward their personal and professional development. If you apply these steps in *your* life, you will not only have healthier relationships, your life will be transformed!

You **can** achieve whatsoever you desire. Everything you want is within your reach! If you have the right mindset and take the right action, you will achieve your goals.

You have the power and now the tools to develop healthy relationships with anyone. This is **your time** to take action toward fulfilling your relationship goals! Please let me know your progress by visiting CoachJamesJustin.com and send me an email!

Notes

What is Healthy Relationship?

Healthy relationship is formed when two or more people develop a strong connection based on mutual respect, trust and support. In healthy relationships each member is *celebrated* rather than *tolerated*.

What are the Signs of an Unhealthy Relationship?

There is no perfect relationship. At times, all relationships will reveal flaws. However, unhealthy relationships will exhibit these characteristics more frequently and lead to stress and pressure that is hard to avoid. Here are some of the signs of unhealthy relationships as noted by the University of Washington Hall Health Center:

- Putting one person before the other by neglecting yourself or your partner.
- Feeling pressure to change who you are for the other person.
- Feeling worried when you disagree with the other person.
- Feeling pressure to quit activities you usually/used to enjoy.
- Pressuring the other person into agreeing with you or changing to suit you better.
- Realizing that one of you has to justify your actions, such as where you go and who you see.

- Recognizing when one partner feels obligated to have sex, or has been forced.
- Having a lack of privacy, and possibly forced to share everything with the other person.
- You or your partner refuses to use safer sex methods.
- Noting that arguments are not settled fairly.
- Experiencing yelling or physical violence during an argument.
- Attempting to control or manipulate each other.
- Noticing that your partner attempts to control how you dress, and criticizes your behaviors.
- Not spending time together.
- Having no common friends, or demonstrating a lack of respect for each other's friends and family.
- Noticing an unequal control of resources such as food, money, home, car, etc.
- Experiencing a lack of fairness and equality.

If you experience some of these characteristics in a relationship, it does not necessarily mean the end of that relationship. They are warning signs that you need to check that relationship and take immediate action for improvement. By recognizing how these characteristics affect you, you can begin to work on improving the negative aspect of an unhealthy relationship. If you need help to improve your relationships visit CoachJamesJustin.com and request a complementary coaching session!

Self-Awareness Questionnaire

Self-awareness is an ongoing process of knowing and accepting who you are. It requires patience and persistence, and the keystone for developing healthy relationships. In any relationship you can only offer who you are and what you have. Therefore, it is necessary to take the time to become self-aware.

Before pursuing any relationship, it is best to know who *you* are. When you are self-aware you are likely to be more confident to developing your purpose. If you want to know yourself, you must invest in yourself. Often, you will reap whatever you sow in your life.

I urge you to take some time to learn about yourself. Remember, you can only give what you have. When you are self-aware, you will be able to manage yourself more efficiently. The more self-aware you are, the more effective you will be in developing healthy relationships as a result of your increased self-esteem.

Completing this questionnaire will help you in your self-awareness process. It will facilitate discovering your purpose, identifying your core values, beliefs, emotional state, strengths, weaknesses and other important information about yourself. I recommend that you take some time to answer these questions as truthfully as you can. If you are unable to answer some of the questions, you can ask a family member or friend to help you.

After completing this questionnaire, it is important to reflect on your answers. You can review them as often as possible and make changes accordingly. When you identify the key aspects of your life, you can then develop a plan for improvement. You will also be in a better equipped to develop healthy relationships.

These are some of the questions I answered as part of my self-awareness analysis. You may find them useful in your own analysis. If you answer them honestly you will know more about yourself than the majority of people in the world. Since self-awareness is an ongoing process, I suggest that you review your answers periodically. You may realize that you progressively grow in awareness.

1) Who am I and where did I come from?

2) What is my definite purpose in life? How can I use my purpose to serve humanity? What is the plan to fulfill my purpose?

3) Am I spiritually, psychologically and physically healthy to achieve my purpose? If so, how? If not, why not, and what can I do to change?

4) What are my core values and beliefs? How are they governing my life? What is the action plan to resolve any internal conflicts?

5) Overall, am I happy with myself? If not, why? What is the plan to fix that?

6) What are my greatest weaknesses and fears? What is the plan to manage/eliminate them without blaming God and others? How can I profit from these changes?

7) How do I manage negative energy, discouraging thoughts and destructive feelings? How do I shield myself from such disturbances?

8) Do I see the silver lining in the cloud, or do I complain when I don't get my way in life? If so, why?

9) Am I easily influenced by others against my own thoughts, feelings or judgments? If so, why? What am I going to do to change that?

10) What is my support system? Are my relationships "mutually beneficial?" If not, why? What is the plan to fix that?

3 Tips to Maximize Your Self-Esteem

We were all born with high self-esteem, and our self-esteem continues to develop throughout life. Self-esteem plays a major role in our success, joy and happiness. It empowers us to pursue our dreams and goals, and enjoy everyday life.

> *"Confidence has nothing to do with what you look like. If you obsess over that, you'll end up being disappointed in yourself all the time. Instead, high self-esteem comes from how you feel in any moment. So walk into a room acting like you're in charge, and spend your energy on making the people around you happy."*
>
> Marian Seldes

Self-esteem is a person's overall assessment of their worth. It is one's belief, values, abilities and self-respect. The Mayo Clinic describes self-esteem as "...*your overall opinion of yourself—how you feel about your abilities and limitations. When you have healthy self-esteem, you feel good about yourself and see yourself as deserving the respect of others. When you have low self-esteem, you put little value on your opinions and ideas. You might constantly worry that you aren't good enough.*"

1. Commit to personal and professional development.

2. Focus on your strengths, while managing your weaknesses.

3. Help others. This practice empowers you to maintain a happier and balanced life.

We can all improve our self-esteem. As you continue to practice the tips provided, your self-esteem will be maximized and your life will be transformed.

For more tips to boost your self-esteem, or to request a complementary coaching session visit CoachJamesJustin.com

3 Tips to Boost Your Confidence

> *"With realization of one's own potential and self-confidence in one's ability, one can build a better world."*
>
> Dalai Lama

Self-confidence is one of the keys to greater success and happiness. Your confidence begins in your mind. It empowers you to utilize your skills and abilities more efficiently. Your confidence is developed by believing and practicing what you are great at doing.

Confidence is a feeling and a belief that you can do something well or achieving a goal. People with high self-confidence believe in their knowledge, abilities and skills, and use their resources to achieve defined goals. When you believe in yourself you'll have the confidence to set, pursue and achieve your goals.

1. Stop Comparing Yourself
- You're unique and you're special!
- Love and accept yourself if you want to gain the confidence required to achieve your goals.
- In the words of Oscar Wilde: *"Be yourself. Everyone else is already taken."*

2. Relax, You're Not Alone
- We all have low self-confidence in some area of our lives.
- Identify the area you want to improve.

- Get the help you need to master it.
- Never stop developing and growing. The path to success requires continuous growth.

3. Do What You Love
- Life is too short to waste your precious time, money and energy on meaningless activities. Invest your efforts on what you love and what brings you the greatest returns.
- Take one step per day toward achieving and enjoying what you love in your life.
- Share and help others do the same. When you help and share constructively, it builds confidence and significance.

We all can boost our confidence. That's good news! It does not matter how low our confidence is right now; we can always improve it. It's a matter of making the choice and following the simple steps outlined in this section. I encourage you to take the necessary time and effort to improve yourself and live your life to its fullest.

Finding Significance

Significance means feeling worthy of attention and importance. Finding significance in your life plays a major role in becoming self-aware. People who find significance in life are happier than those who are unaware of who they are and **whose** they are. They often feel that they do not belong. Finding significance will give you the positive perspective to understand and enjoy your life.

Significance is a vital subject that deserves its own book. However, I could not write chapters on self-discovery without at least mentioning the importance of this concept.

When you find your significance, you find your purpose.

Self-awareness is meaningless without significance. Life without significance is like accumulating enormous wealth and never enjoying it. It is like gaining the world and losing your life. Life is meaningless without discovering its significance.

When you find your significance you find your purpose. We all need a purpose, for without a purpose we would be merely existing and not living. Purpose is a calling or a motivating force to move forward. The truth is, if you seek your purpose you will eventually find it.

The purpose of your life must be pursued diligently in order for it to become a reality.

The process of self-fulfillment is an art. It is the ability to accept yourself, enjoy life and live in peace and contentment according to your purpose. I believe that significance is the process of discovering who you are, accepting who you are and pursuing your purpose and passion. The purpose of your life must be pursued diligently in order for it to become a reality.

Motivation: Why We Do What We Do—an overview on the 6 Basic Human Needs

There's always a reasons why we act the way we do. One essential factor is our **needs**. The more we understand our needs, our thoughts, our feelings and actions, the more we can influence our life. The process of understanding who we are is a major key to our success, joy and happiness.

As a child I was fascinated about why people think, feel and act the way they do. Why some people pursue opportunities that lead to greater success, joy and happiness, while others consistently ignore those same opportunities that can transform their lives forever. I was curious to know why some people sacrificed their lives for others, while some will murder a family member, a friend or a stranger for their own personal gain. Why people such as Jesus Christ, Mother Teresa, Nelson Mandela and Dr. Martin Luther King, Jr. sacrificed their lives for a cause and the greater good of humanity?

It is my passion to understand the human spirit, psychology and behaviors that led me to earn my master's degree in the field of counseling, and dedicate my life to coaching, speaking and helping people like **YOU**!

While each person is unique, we all share similar basic needs. And most of our behaviors are driven by those needs.

According to Abraham Maslow there are six basic human needs that drive our thoughts, feelings and actions. They are as follows:

The 6 Basic Human Needs
Abraham Maslow

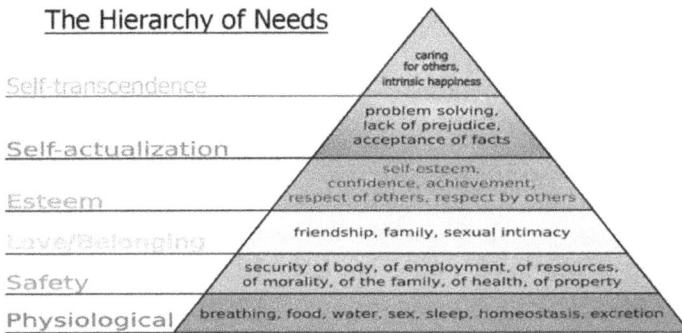

The Hierarchy of Needs

Self-transcendence — caring for others, intrinsic happiness

Self-actualization — problem solving, lack of prejudice, acceptance of facts

Esteem — self-esteem, confidence, achievement, respect of others, respect by others

Love/Belonging — friendship, family, sexual intimacy

Safety — security of body, of employment, of resources, of morality, of the family, of health, of property

Physiological — breathing, food, water, sex, sleep, homeostasis, excretion

1. Physiological
These needs are required for our basic survival, and include air, water, food and sleep.

2. Safety
- Personal security
- Financial security
- Health and well-being

3. Love and Belonging
This need is interpersonal and involves feelings   of belonging, connection, love and Intimacy.

4. Esteem
All humans have a need to feel respected. This includes the need for self-esteem, self-respect and self-confidence. Esteem encompasses the typical human desire to be accepted and valued by others. People often engage in a profession or hobby to gain recognition. These activities give the person a sense of contribution or value.

5. Self-Actualization
This level of need refers to what a person's full potential is and the realization of that potential. Maslow describes this level as the desire to accomplish everything that one can, to become the most that one can be. According to Maslow, *"What a man can be, he must be."*

6. Self-Transcendence
In his later years, Maslow added the sixth need. He realized that the "self" only finds its actualization in its giving to some higher goal outside oneself, in altruism and spirituality.

Tony Robbins' philosophy on the basic human needs

Robins formulated his own list of 6 basic human needs. He believes that the mastery of these needs is essential to personal growth and motivation. Here are his 6 basic human needs:

1. Certainty
We all want comfort and pleasure, and do our best to avoid pain. We want certainty...that the car will start, our family and friends will be there for us and we'll have enough money to maintain our lifestyle.

2. Uncertainty/Variety
The need for the unknown and changes. At the same time, we want certainty, we also crave variety. This process makes life interesting and exciting.

3. Significance
The need to feel that we are unique, important and special. Deep down we all want to be important, popular and valued.

4. Connection/Love
A strong feeling of love and closeness with someone and with something. We want to feel part of a community where we are cared for and cared about.

5. Growth
The need to expend our capacity, capability or understanding. It's the need to become better, to improve our skills, to develop and to excel.

6. Contribution
The need to serve, to help, to share, to give, to inspire, to empower and to support others. The desire to help others make the world a better place.

The basic needs discussed in this section offer only a psychological view on human behaviors and personality. Review these needs as often as possible to better understand *your* needs. When you understand your needs and take proactive steps to meet them, it will help you develop new patterns that lead to lasting fulfillment, success, joy and happiness.

No one can please everyone

In pursuing healthy relationships, it is crucial to realize that you simply cannot please everyone. Therefore, I recommend that you choose your friends wisely. You will go crazy trying to please everyone. The following story from Aesop's Fables illustrates this point.

"The Man, the Boy and the Donkey" translated by G.F. Townsend

A man and his son were going with their donkey to market. As they were walking alongside the donkey, a countryman passed them and said: "You fools, what's a donkey for but to ride upon it?" So the man put the boy on the donkey and they went on their way. But soon they passed a group of men, one of whom said: "See that lazy youngster? He lets his father walk while he rides."

So the man ordered his boy to get off and got on himself. But they hadn't gone far when they passed two women, one of whom said to the other, "Shame on that lazy lout to let his poor little son trudge along."

Well, the man didn't know what to do, but at last he took his boy up before him on the donkey. By this time, they had arrived in the town, and the passers-by began to jeer and point at them. The man stopped and asked what they were scoffing at. The men said, "Aren't you ashamed of yourself for overloading that poor donkey with you and your son's hulking weight?"

The man and boy got off and tried to think what to do. They thought and they thought, until at last they cut down a pole, tied the donkey's feet to it, and raised the pole and the donkey to their shoulders. They went along amidst the laughter of all who met them, until they came to a bridge. Suddenly the donkey, getting one of his feet loose, kicked out and caused the boy to drop his end of the pole. In the struggle, the donkey fell over the bridge, and with his fore-feet still tied to the pole, drowned.

The moral of the story: You cannot please everyone. If you are trying to please everyone, you will end up pleasing no one.

How to Build Rapport in Relationship

In choosing the right people with which to develop healthy relationship, it's important to have a pool of people to choose from. Start with a group of people that you interact with on a regular basis; that you can build rapport with. Rapport can be immediately established upon first meeting someone. If you want to develop new relationships, it is important that you position yourself in settings where you can meet like-minded people.

What is Rapport?

Rapport is a term derived from the French word rapporteur, or reporter, which means to bring back a message. It is the process of building mutual trust and respect characterized by a harmonious and mutual relationship. Proper rapport takes place when two or more people are in sync or on the same thought vibration or wavelength, because they feel similar and relate well to each other.

Why Rapport is Necessary in Developing Healthy Relationships

Rapport helps us to connect with like-minded people. Generally, people become friends with those they like and have proper rapport with. People are more receptive to engage in friendships with people like themselves. It is a universal law of attraction. It can help us to attract those who are of similar mindsets. When this concept is well understood, it can be used to build proper rapport. For example, I can tell in minutes if an interviewee is in rapport with me by watching how they mirror and reciprocate my body language, as well as other nonverbal cues. In everyday life, building rapport can help with persuasion, sales, marketing, teamwork, dating and communicating more effectively with your loved ones.

The Benefits of Rapport

- Rapport provides the fertile soil for fruitful relationships.
- Rapport reduces tension and awkwardness in developing healthy, mutual relationships.
- Rapport provides the comfort, respect and trust to address miscommunication, as required in building healthy relationships.
- Rapport allows the audience to be more open to listen to a speaker attentively.
- Rapport crystallizes the mind and the heart, creating a *buyer* out of a *potential buyer*.

5 Tips to Build Rapport in your Relationships

1. Mirror body language
When connected with people, we tend to mirror their posture and body movements. It is a natural process that takes place subconsciously. We may not even be aware that we are mirroring if we are trained. If you want to practice mirroring, wait 10 seconds and then shift your body in the same way as the other person.

2. Gestures
Use the same hand gestures they use, but only when it's your turn to talk. This will create a connection between you and the other party.

3. Facial Expressions
Match their facial expressions instantly. If they raise their eyebrows, raise yours to acknowledge their emotion.

4. Head Nods
When they nod their head, nod yours instantly to signal agreement or affirmation.

5. Mimic their tonality
Use a similar tone of voice. If they are speaking loudly, speak loudly. If they are whispering, try your best to whisper or talk quietly. The goal is to match the tonality as much as possible to create a connection.

Tips for Healthy Dating

Looking for a date? You are not alone! There are many single people worldwide looking for Mr. or Mrs. "Right." Hence, dating websites are becoming big money-making businesses.

Dating is a form of courtship—including social activities—done between two people with the aim of assessing compatibility as a partner in an intimate relationship, or as a spouse. It is the process of finding a soul mate. In the right settings, close friends often make great soul mates. Here are some important tips for healthy dating:

1. Get to know yourself and be yourself

It is important to continue to work on yourself, for you will only attract who you are. As you grow personally, you'll have more confidence to accept yourself and attract the right person you want to date. Here are some positive affirmations for personal growth:

- I am created in the image and likeness of God.
- I am beautiful!
- I am blessed!
- I am successful!
- I live in abundance!
- I healthy and wealthy!
- I am highly favored, greatly blessed and deeply loved!
- Favor and prosperity follows me everywhere I go!

- I am loved by God and those around me.
- Everything I touch multiplies and grows.
- I am generous because I live in the overflow.
- I am confident and purpose driven.

2. Define why you want date that person

It is important to have a definite purpose for your dating. If you do not have a purpose, you will get lost in the emotional process and come out with no mate. Your life is too precious to be wasted with those who will not appreciate nor accept you.

3. Decide who you want to date and where you will find the person

In you want to develop healthy relationship, you must become selective. Don't just date anyone, pick the one you want to date and pursue it.

Also, you must select the right setting where you will find your potential date. You have to be strategic where you go and where you meet people. Since everything produces after its kind, you most likely will find the same kind of people in similar settings. For example, the rich often hang out with other rich people. Therefore, it you want to date a rich person, you must go where they are. I cannot tell you specifically where you can find your soul mate, but you can pray for God's guidance like I did.

You are a unique individual, and my settings may not work for you. Therefore, I urge you to find settings where you can be comfortable, and where you can be yourself. My advice is for you to go where you are *celebrated* rather than *tolerated*. Some popular places to meet new people include church, school, work, fitness centers, dating websites, weddings and other social events. Your current friends can also introduce to their friends, so ask for help.

4. Get to know the person you are dating
Take some time to get to know your date. Go out and get to know each other. Take it one step at a time. Don't let a relationship move too fast. Romantic affairs that begin too soon and in a frenzy way, frequently burn themselves out.

5. Respect
Remember that respect precedes love. Healthy relationship requires mutual respect. If you feel that you are not being respected, address it immediately or walk away.

6. Be patient
At the early stage of dating, avoid too many contacts. Don't text, email or call too often on the phone or give the other person an opportunity to get tired of you.

7. Be wise
Take your time before sharing personal information. Don't discuss your personal flaws in great detail in the early stage of dating. No matter how warm and accepting your friend may be, any great revelation of low self-esteem or embarrassing weaknesses can be

fatal to a new relationship. Also, don't be too quick to reveal your desire to get married on a first date. This makes you look too desperate.

7 Tips for Healthy Marriage

Marriage is a process that requires ongoing discovery and maintenance. One of my mentors wrote a book about marriage that I highly recommend all couples read: "Driving the Nail Home" by Reverend Jean Toth. I also recommend the following 7 tips for marriage development. (They helped me in *my* marriage):

1. **Play and laugh together.**

2. **Keep on learning together.**

3. **Apologize often, and forgive even more.**

4. **Never go to sleep mad at each other.**

5. **Talk, Talk, Talk...about everything!**

6. **Manage your money together.**

7. **Build intimacy and have sex often.**

You do not have to wait until you find Mr. or Mrs. "Right" to start planning for a healthy marriage. You can start today by working on yourself. Mr. or Mrs. "Right" may be in front of you. However, you may be blinded by your own issues.

This is the reason I recommend that you work on yourself to prepare for meeting Mr. or Mrs. "Right." For example, I started praying for my soul mate at the age of 14, and I did not meet my wife until I was 18.

To maintain a healthy marriage, I attended several marriage conferences, Sunday school classes for couples and even led some of the classes with my wife. My wife and I still listen to teaching CDs on the subject of marriage and how to be successful as a married couple. We even developed a coaching program called The Copreneurs: How to Achieve Success Together as a Couple. As part of my marriage, I am reading several books listed in the reference section of this book. I recommend that you add these resources to your library, and regularly practice what you have learned. Remember, I stated that a meaningful marriage requires maintenance. I know this is true, since I noticed that my marriage is not effective when a tune-up is required. Therefore, my wife and I made it our focus to develop our relationship.

If you are struggling in your marriage I encourage you to not give up on your dream of a *meaningful* marriage. It is always too early to quit. You may be only three feet away from your dream. Christian psychiatrist Dr. Paul D. Meier says that there are "...*Only three choices for any person involved in an unhappy marriage: (1) Get a divorce—the greatest cop-out, and by far the most immature choice; (2) Tough out the marriage without working to improve it—another immature decision, but not quite as irresponsible as divorce; and (3) Maturely face up to personal hang-ups, and choose to build an intimate marriage out of the existing one—the only real mature choice to make.*" No matter how bad your marriage may be, it is never too late for God's intervention. All things are possible with God and those who believe. If both parties are willing, there is always hope to restore the marriage. I advise that you continue to pray for your marriage, and seek help from loving people or a professional counselor.

Justin's Listening Scale

> *"When you talk, you are only repeating what you already know. But, if you listen, you may learn something new."*
> Dalai Lama

Are you an effective listener? This scale will help you assess your listening skills. Everyone has the ability to become a better listener. As you determine your score in this listening skill scale, you will be able to develop a strategic plan for improvement. As you know from reading this book, communication is an important key in developing healthy relationships and in success in life. Effective communication is primarily nonverbal. The more you can listen attentively, the more effective you will become in communicating with people. If you want to become an effective communicator, you must start by developing your listening skills.

Instruction: After reading each statement, use the scale to indicate how often these sentences are true for you. Be honest!

Rating: 0 = Never; 2 = Rarely; 5 = Occasionally
7 = Often   10 = Always

1. My friends tell me that I am a good listener.

2. I listen twice before I speak.

3. I look beyond the words of the speaker; I focus on the body language, tone of voice and other non-verbal expressions, and ask questions for clarification before I respond.

4. To ensure that I am listening, I use listening signs such as ok, yes, gee, I see...

5. I listen to people with an open mind.

6. Overall, I consider myself a good listener.

7. I often daydream while listening to people.

8. Before my family members and friends complete their statements, I often have the answers to their problems.

9. I often get distracted and miss much of what is being said in a lecture. 10. I often talk more than I listen.

Scoring:

Add the numbers, then divide that total by 10 to calculate your overall listening skills score. For example, a score of 89 is 8.9.

Meaning of your score:

8-10: You are a good listener.

5-7: You are average to above average. (Most people fall in this category.) .

Less than 5: You might have relationship difficulties due to poor listening skills.

We all can improve our listening skills with planning, preparation, practice and commitment. Once you have your listening score, I highly recommend that you develop a strategic action plan for improvement. It will be helpful to read this book as often as possible to get a refresher course on the subject of listening and communication. For personal and professional coaching, visit CoachJamesJustin.com!

About The Author

A born leader, James Justin hasn't let any obstacles stand in the way of his success. And he has the skills to make sure your obstacles are broken and no longer stand in your way.

"It is my passion to inspire and help you transform your life! This passion led me to earn my master's degree in the field of counseling, and for over 20 years I have dedicated my life to helping people like YOU achieve EXTRAORDINARY results!"

James is a speaker, minister, author, life coach and entrepreneur. He earned his Master of Social Work (MSW) degree from Boston College, and his Bachelor of Social Work (BSW) degree from Eastern Nazarene College.

James worked as a Professional Counselor for the State of Florida for seven years prior to pursuing his passion and his dream: to help and make an impact in the private sector.

In 2011, James and his wife, Dr. Lauretta Justin, co-authored and published their first book, "Express Yourself." This title and other products are available at CoachJamesJustin.com.

James and Dr. Lauretta are the proud parents of three incredible and active boys, and spend the majority of their free time focusing on "the boys."

James is committed to helping create transformational growth with each and every one of his clients. To contact James, visit CoachJamesJustin.com.

7 Steps to Develop
HEALTHY RELATIONSHIPS
With Anyone

Did you know that healthy relationships are an essential link to your success, happiness and wellbeing? Knowing how to attract, select and nurture healthy relationships within your circle of life will enable you to utilize these relationships as an invaluable source of inspiration, support and strength. These healthy relationships will help you to achieve your goals!

In healthy relationships each member is *CELEBRATED* rather than *TOLERATED*.

This book reveals the vital 7 steps you must know to attract and maintain healthy relationships with anyone in your personal and business life. If you allow the wrong people in your circle of life, it will have a negative impact on your path to continued success. This book is your key to create the healthy relationships that will unlock your dynamic potential. The steps outlined in this book are life changing. If you read this book and apply its principles, you will not only enjoy BETTER RELATIONSHIPS, you will have a BETTER LIFE!

WHAT READERS ARE SAYING:

"Our relationship is incredible thanks to James!" —Joe and Vanessa Roberts

"I'm in a better place in my life since I learned how to develop healthy relationships. Thanks James!" —Allison Matthews

"My relationships with my employees improved as a result of reading this book. Everyone is happier in the office and we're increasing profits! I recommend this book to anyone who wants to grow their business." —Michael Alexander

CoachJamesJustin.com